THE 'LANGUAGE OF ROCK 'N' ROLL'

About The Authors

YOUNG AND MOODY first met on a European Tour over ten years ago and have since written over one hundred songs together. They have also recorded a couple of albums and several singles as Young and Moody and have for nine years played as members of the temporary almost legendary John Coghlan's Diesel Band.

BOB YOUNG was born in Basingstoke in 1945 and was raised there as a baby who enjoyed filling his nappies underneath the next door neighbour's Austin Seven, as a schoolboy who only enjoyed football because the pitch backed onto the girls' school playground, as an apprentice tool-maker who liked his tool, and as a folksinger who found the blues when no folk came to see him.

In 1968 he moved to London where he met and joined the group Status Quo as their tour manager/harmonica player and songwriter. Having travelled the world several times over with them he quite recently stopped touring to concentrate more on his writing. As well as Quo classics such as 'Caroline', 'Down Down', 'Living On An Island' and many more songs, he has co-written several plays for television (he is currently high on list of London's unsuccessful playwrights), a television series for comedian Jim Davidson, a book of poetry and, with John Shearlaw, a humorous history of Status Quo called *Again and Again*.

MICKY MOODY was born in Middlesbrough but denies that it was his fault. This geographical location was occupied by the subject for the first seventeen years of his life with an attitude probably best described by the famous Eccles: "Everybody's got to be somewhere."

An early love for football gradually gave way to an almost obsessive interest in all things connected with the guitar, which included a long period of private tuition. This led to the forming of a group with classmate Paul Rodgers, and the inevitable exodus down the A1 to London.

After many many thousands of miles, stamped passports, and bands like Juicy Lucy and Whitesnake to sessions for all kinds of artistes, Micky is still a muso at heart and a man of the road (even if it's just crossing one to reach the pub).

THE 'LANGUAGE OF ROCK 'n' ROLL'

BOB YOUNG & MICKY MOODY

Sidgwick & Jackson

London

First published in Great Britain in 1985
by Sidgwick and Jackson Limited.

Copyright © 1985 by Bob Young and Micky Moody

ISBN 0-283-99239-5
Printed in Great Britain by
A. Wheaton & Co. Ltd., Exeter
for Sidgwick and Jackson Limited
1 Tavistock Chambers, Bloomsbury Way
London WC1A 2SG

Acknowledgements

The authors would like to thank Robert Fletcher and Martin G. Jowers for their illustrations, Zak Starkey for the original crossword, Mother Young for board, lodging and chips, and wives, children and friends for their patient support.

Eternal gratitude is also extended to everybody in the rock music world whose influences have, unbeknown to them, helped enormously in the compilation of this book.

Preface

Every culture creates its own language, and rock and roll is certainly no exception. Spanning just over three decades, the language, much influenced by the black American attitude towards enjoyment, is still relatively young. Music itself has of course been around a little longer, and no doubt the musicians of the day used words and sayings peculiar to them. It is extremely doubtful, for example, that the conversation in Amadeus Mozart's dressing room, at the conclusion of his performance, was on the lines of:

'Hey, Mozy baby, what a blinding gig that was. Did you see those two rods with the strapping bristols in the front row? If we can pull them back later and swag the night porter to keep stumm, I reckon we would top that massage we had in Tokyo last week.'

'Sweet man, but the dawn patrol's out the window for me.'

The 'beat boom' of the early sixties, heralded by the Beatles and the Rolling Stones while Elvis Presley succumbed to second-rate movie-making, forced the world to accept a new culture – the 'rock culture'. Young people had decided to have some say in the way that their lives were run, and for the first time in history they were at the forefront of modern technological mass-media appeal through television, radio, and popular recordings.

In the past, music had been written either to be performed by virtuoso players and appreciated by an audience, or as a background to human emotions. With the advent of the rock culture it took on a much more participatory role; audiences became more physically and emotionally involved, due mainly to the hypnotic and infectious rhythmic pulse generated by rock and roll. This original musical excitement gradually, and naturally, conceived a new form of expression, the serious lyric.

9

The aural and physical form of rock entertainment has become the mainstay of popular music and seems destined to stay, though as an art form it has had no shortage of criticism from the many who refuse to accept it as a major force, not only on the economies of most major countries, but as an essential, serious and healthy means of expression by the young and young at heart. The content of modern rock music is varied, to say the least, and caters for every individual.

Over the last thirty-odd years, many people from all classes of life have become involved with rock music and the rock scene in general. The development of its communicative dialogue comes from them, and their influence runs throughout this book. But it must be stressed at this point that the initial inspiration for writing the book came purely from that most treasured of human characteristics, humour. This most valuable attribute is essential to all rock personnel as a means of combating stress, disappointment, and mental instability.

No compilation of rock and roll colloquialisms can ever be complete, as every day new combinations of characters will find new expressions that are exclusive to the lifestyle. Just as the Cockneys developed their own inimitable rhyming slang, with new and contemporary meanings being added almost daily, so the language of rock and roll will continue to evolve and develop.

What follows is an insight into the language drawn from the authors' professional and innocent experiences, some of which Herr Mozart may have shared, though he would surely have expressed them differently.

We have also included a selection of anecdotes from various celebrities and characters in the music business (see the list at the end of the book). Some of their stories are even more outlandish than our own!

We are grateful to the Nordoff-Robbins Music Therapy organization for their assistance in the collation of these.

BOB YOUNG and MICKY MOODY

AGENT Formerly known as Mr 10 per cent, his role in the entertainment world was to force his clients into an early grave through overwork and then revel in their martyrdom. Times have changed though, and due to a mass revolt some time in the sixties he now has to settle for just the occasional nervous breakdown.

The modern-day agent tends to conduct a lot of his business over lunch. So, aware of his bulging waistline, he prefers to skip the meal and get pissed instead. It's worth noting that 'lunch', as far as an agent is concerned, can be consumed at any time of the morning, day or night.

'Agent'

AIR HOSTESS   Uniformed women rate highly in the sexual fantasies of most men, and as far as musicians are concerned air hostesses surely come out top of the list because (a) they are generally attractive and not with their boyfriends, (b) aeroplane vibrations are the most conducive to unexpected attacks of traveller's marrow (see Traveller's Marrow), and (c) because comparatively speaking uniformed railway porters never look the same no matter how great the train vibration or big the traveller's.

Generally speaking, air hostesses will welcome the arrival of rock bands on board because they can make a pleasant change from the average day-to-day passenger. Occasionally, though, they have to suffer rowdy and abusive entourages who, mainly due to an excessive amount of alcohol, indulge in childish pranks such as gaffa taping (see Gaffa Tape) mirrors to the tops of their shoes in order to get a better look up the hostess's skirt, or throwing cucumber at the heads of Korean choir girls sitting further up front (for further information on this see chapters on flying in *Status Quo – The Authorised Biography* by John Shearlaw and *Status Quo – Again and Again* by Bob Young and J. Shearlaw both published by Sidgwick and Jackson).

Smarmy tour managers (see Tour Managers) often indulge in a most predictable form of chatting-up which generally includes the promise of free tickets to the next performance of 'his' band. His rank has now of course risen to that of executive producer and his line of chat centres mainly on his next meeting with the head of the group's record company and his plans to enlarge his swimming pool at the mansion he shares with Jacqueline Bisset.

Relationships between rock stars and air hostesses are usually short-lived simply because of the contradictory itineraries of both parties.

AIR STEWARD   Someone who *would* appreciate you putting a mirror on your shoe and looking up his trouser leg.

AMICABLE   As in 'the split was amicable'. Also known as the sack.

'Air Hostess'

ARROGANCE An attitude formerly associated with Teutonic social climbers, but now put into contemporary use by immature and disrespectful rock stars.

ARSEHOLE Nearly everybody at some time or another.

ARTISTE The dictionary defines this term as a person who is an 'expert in some art', but with reference to some of the characters featured in this book, this might not apply.

'When I first went out to Radio Luxembourg, which was the first job I had in radio, I went as a newsreader, not as a disc jockey. I used to read bulletins every hour from 7.30 p.m. until the early hours of the morning. The very first one I had to read was a story about a typhoid epidemic in Italy. It was a very serious story, about 700 people had been hospitalized, including quite a few British tourists, and some had died. I read out the details of the epidemic and then there was this line which really crippled me. It said, "Italian Health Authorities investigating the disaster say that it was almost certainly caused by an ice-cream salesman washing his utensils in the River Po." Paul Burnett choked over his coffee in the background and I just broke up – and this was my first news bulletin in my very first job. I got a terrible letter from the general manager Geoffrey Everitt threatening me with the sack. Then three weeks later I did it again. This was 1968 and there had been a lot of criticism of Concorde and the fact that its inaugural flight was about eighteen months late. And there was some talk that the aircraft was unsafe because they were rushing it through as a result of the criticisms. Anyway, I had to read a bulletin about the inaugural flight, and it began: "Today the maiden flight of Concorde was floorless. . ." I had visions of Concorde travelling up the runway on all these little legs, or at best people sitting there with this incredible draft going up their trousers. I broke up again and I got another letter from Geoffrey Everitt.'

NOEL EDMONDS

14

AUTHORS OF THIS BOOK   See Slightly Cynical.

AUTOGRAPHS   A signature. Autographs have been around for hundreds of years and in fact many have become worth a lot of money to the keen collector. As far as performers are concerned, probably top of the list is Elvis Presley or maybe John Lennon, although without doubt there are many forgeries around. Unscrupulous roadies (see Crew) have been known to forge their boss's signature and sell it, often for less than the price of a pint.

Messages with genuine signatures range from the pleasantly sincere 'Hi baby, get on down and hang loose cos your vibe's with us, man', to 'Piss off you sycophantic sack of shit. Love, severely depressed of Ladbroke Grove'.

BACKGAMMON   A really boring game, played by really boring musicians throughout a really boring tour.

BACK LINE   The 'back line' of amplifiers and speaker cabinets used by the band on stage and originally costing thousands of pounds which is immediately devalued by artistically inclined roadies (see Crew) who insist on covering every square inch of it with spray paint and gaffa tape (see Gaffa Tape).

BACK TO BACK   Two consecutive gigs unreasonably booked so that the crew have to leave directly after one gig and travel nonstop to the next, with little or no sleep, in order to fulfil the band's obligations.

While successful acts spend the night checking out the dawn patrol (see Dawn Patrol), grab five hours' sleep, spend an hour on a plane and arrive at the next gig refreshed and ready to go, the bedraggled crew cheerfully go about their humble duties supported largely by stimulated camaraderie.

Road crews belonging to major rock bands are usually supplied with civilized travelling facilities which normally come in the shape of luxury coaches fitted out with a kitchen, toilet and several beds. Although eight hours' sleep should be guaranteed, when divided between twelve grown children with a shortage of victims, boilers and poo-bums (see appropriate entries), and a strapping amount of beverage blagged (see below) from the artistes' dressing room along

16

with the truck driver's delights, it doesn't really help, as definitely the last one (see Definitely the Last One) is always definitely the order of the day.

Any sensible-thinking crew member who is under the illusion that he can actually undertake a normal night's activity, i.e. sleep, will come in for a dreadful shock. Apart from the general mêlée produced by the travelling disco and social club atmosphere, he will be perpetually disturbed by the pissed individual in the bunk above his, whose constant farts and belches are enough to wake the dead, or kill the living.

BAND ROOMS   See Dressing Rooms.

BEING IN A SUPPORT BAND   Having the distinction of being able to finish your set and be back at the hotel bar before the headline act has gone on stage. Also being in a position (a) to be ripped off by the star attraction, for example having to 'hire' their PA system (see PA) for the next month, or (b) go down better than the headliners because you're bloody good and they're not!

BELGIUM   A graveyard of broken dreams and shattered illusions, and a place to drive through as quickly as possible. Only the emotionally stable should perform there unless accompanied by a deranged adult.

BIBLOSS   A legendary rock disco in Tokyo where visiting Western musicians are given total artistic licence to do, more or less, exactly what they want. Most humble visitors settle for an opportunity to put their libido to the test under an onslaught of feminine encouragement.

BLAG   To acquire something for nothing or even less by usually subtle methods. Items sought after range from women to anything, and are often accompanied by a classic opening line (see Opening Lines).

BLINDER   Fantastic, fabulous, excellent etc., as in 'She was a blinder' or 'It was a blinding gig'.

BLOOZER   An over-emotional sentimentalist.

BLUES   An ethnic form of music of African origins performed originally by Negro slaves in the southern states of
America. The improvisational qualities of this music later
formed the nucleus of what is now called rock and roll, and
has earned fortunes for everybody except Negro slaves.

BLUFFER   A person who plays when really he should listen. Electronic devices can sometimes cover up a genuine
lack of talent but should never be relied on, especially if the
subject is offered a gig with a medieval lute quartet.

BOILER   In general terms, a vessel for boiling water,
resulting inevitably in an excess of steam. In rock and roll
terms, a female vessel for excess sperm, resulting inevitably
in a quick exit (by the donor).

BOOZING   A form of religion to many musicians. A kind
of daily sacrificing of the liver to the god of inebriation.
Someone once stated that you don't need to drink to play
well, but later admitted to being drunk when he said it.

**'I once worked with a bass player and a drummer who got
so wrecked one night that one of them went to sleep in a
bed full of broken egg shells and he never noticed. The
other actually fell asleep under the shower – while it was
still on. He woke up in the morning looking like a merin-
gue, all white and puffy. He's never been the same since.**

ALEXIS KORNER

BOZO   A right clever dick punter (see Punter) who often
starts the evening amongst a crowd of people and ends up
reciting a doleful lament to a packet of crisps.

BOX   (a) The part of a female's anatomy hidden somewhere north of the thighs and south of the naval, as in 'You
should have seen the hairy box on the rod I pulled last night

18

'Bloozer'

after the gig', a common breakfast topic among musos (see Muso). (b) Word used mainly by ageing hippies for the guitar.

BRISTOLS Comes from Bristol cities – titties, tits, breasts, boobs, knockers. (The writers must end this explanation here for humanitarian reasons.)

BRITISH TOUR In the early days of rock band touring, all of the big-name performers were grouped together in various package tours. No, they weren't holidaying together in Benidorm, far from it.

Five or six currently popular acts would travel the length and breadth of the coutry in a coach, often driven by some debauched gambler, and present their act at the local cinema or civic hall.

The 'act' usually consisted of a ten- or fifteen-minute spot (see Spot) and was usually accompanied by a barrage of screams from the invariably female-orientated audience. The top attraction was of courses given a lengthier period of up to twenty-five minutes in which to be screamed at.

Nowadays the British tour is a much more personalized undertaking, and usually revolves around an individual act presenting a show lasting about one and a half hours. A support band (see Support Bands) is often or usually brought in to open the proceedings and their appreciation of the honour is rendered, more often than not, in the shape of a small financial gift to the star band's management 'for the hire of the PA'.

Audiences on a British tour can vary but industrial and depressed areas such as Glasgow, Newcastle and Liverpool have always been regarded as particularly expressive, whereas Eastbourne hasn't.

BULLSHITTING Is (a) the everyday lifestyle of a person who deals in public relations, (b) never having to say you're sorry, (c) saying that this book is volume 2 when it's really volume 1.

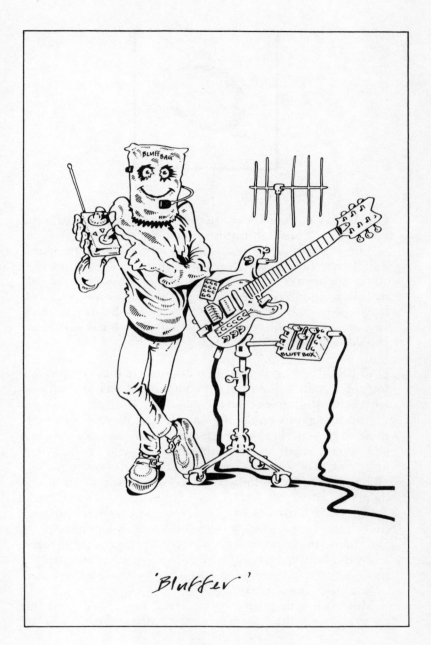

'Bluffer'

CASUALTY   The rock casualty is usually thought of in the past tense, i.e. dead, but this is not always correct.

The stresses and strains confronting the unprepared entertainer (and associates) can sometimes lead to mental states not always experienced by, let's say, your average filing clerk, and excessive drinking and drug abuse can often leave the casualty wondering if he would be happier as, let's say, an average filing clerk. This confused state is lethal and should be avoided at all costs.

CATERERS   A relatively new addition to the rock and roll touring circuit is the catering company, a sort of meals on wheels for up-market road crews.

Appearing only on the big-name tours, they usually comprise of two or three young ladies, some portable cooking equipment, small fridge, eating utensils, and enough food and drink to prevent any member of the road crew from actually having to spend his per diems (see PDs) on such mundane pleasures.

Catering companies and road crews, after initial introductions, usually regard each other with a professional respect, and due to the heavy work schedule have little time to forge any kind of romantic attachment. Physical relationships, however, are sometimes sought after by band lechers and occasionally come to fruition.

Musicians killing time between the soundcheck and the show are, with the crew boss's permission, allowed to enter the temporary kitchen and be served a stale cracker or a finger of Coca-Cola, but once away from official scrutiny can often obtain leftovers, or even a beer.

With the passing of time a favoured band member will be accepted by the crew and allowed to dine with them, sharing the culinary delights and highbrow conversations so prevalent on these occasions.

Choice of food ranges from full breakfast to cauliflower cheese, and appreciation is normally rendered via the anal passage, in the form of a loud Lionel (see Lionels).

CHINNING The ancient art of physical self-expression which is often bestowed upon people of a disagreeable nature. This activity requires the sudden upward thrust of the arm, together with a clenched fist, to make contact with the opponent's anatomy, preferably his face. Many journalists, people with ego problems, habitués of discotheques, and even human beings are often the hapless victims of the habitual chinner, who can appear in almost any shape or form, most notably that of a roadie, and more often than not that of a musician.

'Chinning!'

CLICKER A hand-held, easily concealed counting machine operated by a band representative to check the number of people paying to enter a gig. This device is normally used on percentage-agreed bookings and/or when the promoter may take advantage of the band's trust and claim at the end of the night that there were many less in than actually were. Obviously at large-capacity, all-ticket venues such as the Wembley Stadium this particular method of keeping a tally could prove a little difficult, especially if the clicker is forgotten and the representative has to revert to the original system of counting up to ten as the punters enter and then passing a matchstick from one hand to the other. With 90,000 people coming through the gate this would require 9,000 matches which would look not only conspicuous but very silly.

CLOTH CAPS AND TRILBYS A game invented by a well-known British soul band (featuring a black singer) in the late sixties. It was based on the assumption that the band in question would be driving through the town of Oldham on a Saturday afternoon.

The game had two basic components: (1) the number of cloth caps versus trilby-style hats worn by the masculine gender known to frequent the main shopping area of Oldham on a Saturday between the hours of 1.30 and 4.30 p.m. (2) sufficient band members awake enough to compete.

Once underway, the game could turn into an unforgettable experience, especially if one struck lucky at 'cloth-cap corner', a local shrine erected originally to pay homage to the war dead, but visited now by very old men who like to talk about the war dead and rate-capping.

This particular vantage point has often, unbeknowingly, awarded nine points to the self-elected 'cloth-cap team', whilst the masochistically chosen 'trilby team' look forward with dubious anticipation to a good turn-out of ageing henpecked husbands who tend to favour trilby headwear.

Needless to say, the northern preference for honouring tradition in headwear always won through, and the cloth-cap team was always victorious.

24

'Contract'

CONTRACT   An ordinary piece of paper with a lot of extraordinary demands on it. Offered to 99 per cent of mostly honest and reliable musicians, it gives a new meaning to the word 'mistrust'. Compiled mainly from obscure legal anecdotes, it is designed to completely confuse the average day-to-day tortured artiste.

CREW   The road crew. Known in the past as roadies, and nowadays liable to become extremely irate and offended if referred to as such.

Roadies still exist, of course, working tirelessly for bands and tackling every kind of chore that is thrust upon them. Everything from the laborious packing, unpacking and setting up of the entire group's equipment to the sound-mixing and driving is approached with an enthusiasm bordering on the obsessed.

Most road crew start out in this fashion and then work their way through the ranks to become proficient in one particular field, i.e. sound mixer, monitor mixer, cement mixer, guitar technician(?), keyboard technician(?), lighting engineer, rigger, drum technician(?) etc.

On certain occasions a crew member suffering from delusions of grandeur will outrank his fellow companions to reach the status of tour manager (see Tour Manager).

Modern-day road crews lucky enough to land a gig on a major headline tour can now expect and often demand luxuries unknown in the embryonic days of the rock business – good wages, per diems (see PDs), crew meals, decent hotels and the opportunity sometimes get a reasonable night's sleep (if desired).

These men, and sometimes women, are more often than not true professionals and, it must be said, can be worth their weight in gold.

CYNICAL MUSICIAN   A man with a fine prospect of happiness behind him.

'On my very first tour and very first London date we were out as support and most of RCA were in the theatre to

26

CYNICAL MUSICIAN

cheer us on. I was, of course, terrified, which wasn't helped by learning, an hour before curtain up, that there was no piano. Somehow Maurice Plaquet managed to get a piano to us, we were announced, and on we went, the boys to their instruments and me to the piano which had been placed directly behind a mountain of speakers. I can't say we really captured the audience and I think the moment when I knew the evening was, for us, totally doomed was when the piano pedals fell off. We ploughed on and arrived at the point in our three-quarter-hour act when I introduced the boys in the band – Danny Schogger on keyboards, Kevin Healey on guitar, Andy Pask on bass. . . Applause. We're just settling in to play our final number when a voice in the audience shouts, "And who the hell are you?"'

CATHERINE HOWE

DAFT   A feeling often experienced in euphoric surroundings by silly musicians.

DAWN PATROL   The human, and sometimes sub-human, remains of various band members and crew, quite often found staggering into hotel lobbies at 5 a.m. This miserable entourage then proceeds to various rooms and corridors to continue its decadent activities before grabbing a couple of minutes' sleep prior to the wake-up call (see Wake-up Call).

'Dawn Patrol'

HOTEL POSH

DEFINITELY THE LAST ONE A reference to all manner of things. A phrase often repeated by musicians and roadies alike, usually many times in the same evening.

DEHYDRATION The loss of vital body fluids due to either an excess of alcohol, or an over-zealous lighting technician. The former will result in a hangover, the latter in a bollocking of the guilty lighting operator administered by drained performers.

DESPERATE MAN A person who often bears a certain resemblance to the wibbley-wobbley man (see Wibbley-Wobbley Man), but with deeper pathological problems.

'Many years ago, before everybody was born, I was working as a disc jockey on Radio Luxembourg, and I was only working there because of a phenomenon called "listening figures". I'd taken over a 600,000 listening slot, and three weeks later they were going to elbow me because nobody could understand my Yorkshire accent. Then the listening figures came out and they found I was up to 2,300,000. So they kept me on. That was crisis number one in the life of a new disc jockey. Crisis number two came about ten weeks later when one still wasn't exactly established. Radio Luxembourg decided to alter their policy regarding English-speaking disc jockeys – each record had to be announced in English, German and French, which promptly put about forty disc jockeys out of work (the programmes were very short at that time, some of them only fifteen minutes long). "Great," I told them, "gives me a chance to use my languages." "What languages?" they said. "Japanese, a little bit of Chinese – Cantonese actually, Italian. . ." "Amazing," they said. I rushed back to Leeds with my list of records for the following week and wrote out a script which I gave to this 94-year-old German lady to translate. The problem was that there's two sorts of German, popular and classic, and she wrote classic German. So in the studio I was trying to have a go at this and making a pig's ear of it. What came out was unbelievable

nonsense, and the same with the French, because it's one thing speaking French – which I do quite reasonably – but it's another thing broadcasting French; it just isn't the same. I was saying, "Die drunken Schneikeln, arbeiten sie gut hier" and "Et le prochaine disque c'est un merveilleur, alors, Bob's your uncle". Well, the programme came out and they broadcast it all the way through, and everybody was saying "Fantastic". At the studio the French girl was in hysterics and the German one left the room, couldn't stop laughing and crying. Geoffrey Everitt, the governor of Radio Luxembourg, didn't think it was so funny. I was nobody at the time, I hadn't been on TV or anything, I was a dance hall manager, so I was battling for my life, but being a survivor I managed to persuade him to let me do some Spanish as well. So the following week, there I was with the bollocks German, the upside-down French, and the phrase-book Spanish. I translated little things like "A bird in the hand is worth two in the bush", and the way it came out in Spanish was "It is a surprise pigeon that has a tree thrust up its bum". This was broadcast, and I thought, "Well, I've got one week's wages, I'll settle for just one week's wages." But the Spanish people thought it was great, and once again the French were in hysterics and the Germans on the floor, and that saved my life in the early embryo days of being a disc jockey.'

JIMMY SAVILE

DJs   Disc jockeys. Jocks. Originally simply the person who chose and played records to the public, although nowadays that would be a gross understatement.

One of the first DJs to deliberately aim at taking himself out of the 'person who plays the records' and into 'the celebrity in his own right' was American jock, Murray the K, who had the audacity to call himself 'the Fifth Beatle' when the group arrived for their first US tour. They probably called him a prat when they left.

Many DJs adopt a vocal delivery that has been termed 'mid-Atlantic', but whether or not they were born and bred

32

in the mythical city of Atlantis remains unproven.

In the book *How To Become a DJ and Make Lots of Cash* by the almost legendary Wayne Rhonda (see Image), the author stresses in no uncertain fashion 'the importance of being earnest and faithful right up to the end', especially regarding public appearances. By taking an engagement outside the radio station he can make enough money to open up his own shop and sell all those complimentary albums that record companies send him.

Radio Luxembourg has been broadcasting pop music since pop became pop but reception in the UK (because of geographical distance) has always been plagued with interference. The experience of hearing Western rock music interlaced with Rumanian death marches is not always appreciated.

As some of the anecdotes in this book show, the DJ is not that far removed from the rock/pop artiste in as much as he believes that humour is an important part of rock 'n' roll and a harmless way of relieving the unseen pressures brought on by the irregular hours worked, potential excesses available and continually unpredictable future in a business well known for its 'flavour of the month' attitude.

'Over the last few years I have been much maligned by my fellows here at Radio One who think quite wrongly that I'm a bit of a prankster and get up to no good from time to time. Anyway, a whole crew of them decided it was time to get their own back on me and they hatched an amazing plot which took two days to plan. We were in this hotel in Bristol and at about 4 a.m. I thought I'd go off to bed. Everybody else was still up, even the early bedders. I thought it was strange because some of them were flagging and I wondered why they didn't go to bed. Anyway, I got to my room and there in the bed was this monstrous face. It was a scarecrow, its head lit up with a torch. It looked really evil. I put the light on, startled out of my wits, and the place was like a manger. It was covered with straw and smelled of manure – absolutely horrible. But not just manure, there was something else. It took me about an hour to locate the kippers. After taking the bedroom apart piece by piece I eventually realized that the kipper smell must be coming from somewhere warm, because it got stronger and stronger. There were four radiators in the room. I took them all apart and behind each one I found a rotten, stinking kipper. So I cleared up the straw and I cleared up the kippers. I was on my last legs because it was now about 5.15 a.m. and I had to get up at 6. I'll just have three-quarters of an hour's sleep, I thought, so I jumped into bed and the bed collapsed with me folded up in the middle, and there was more straw in the bed. I'm just going to lie here and not move, I thought, but I needed an alarm call in case I fell asleep. So I picked up the phone and as I clamped it to my ear I discovered there was manure and straw all over it as well. The phone was dead anyway. I thought I'd just lie there for half an hour, trying not to go to sleep. But then water started running in the bathroom. It wasn't just dribbling, it was pouring, so I thought there must be somebody in there. In the dark I got up and stealthily crept over to the bathroom. I wanted to surprise whoever was in there. I carefully put my hand on the door handle and then pushed as hard as I could with my full weight. The swines had taken the hinges off and I fell in on top of the bath. Really painful for me and also for the dozen chickens in the bathroom, lined up in the bath, one in the sink, one sitting on the loo. It was a real shock. Chickens squawking, beaks everywhere, feathers everywhere. Of course we'd had a few glasses of lemonade earlier, so I was standing there talking to this chicken, the one in the sink, saying, "You're rather an attractive chicken, as chickens go of course." Outside Simon Bates and Noel Edmonds were killing themselves. I heard this noise of shrieking and rushed outside. Simon made it to his bedroom but Noel didn't, and I pursued him round the hotel for about ten minutes, me yelling after him, people coming out of their rooms and yelling at both of us as a naked Noel Edmonds streaked past them with a naked me in hot pursuit. I got no sleep that night. But you wait till next time we go out!'

MIKE READ

DO-GOODERS   Do-gooders in the show-biz world have little in common with their counterparts at the charitable end of the scale. This kind of person is not interested in raising funds for a particular cause, only in raising his prominence in whatever surroundings he finds himself. He usually has a very vague connection with the entertainment world, quite often a mini-cab driver suffering from delusions of grandeur, or maybe an ex-roadie who once met Francis Rossi.

Whatever the do-gooder's limited experience is, the poor down-at-heel performer will find out over the next two hours as he tries desperately to enjoy his quiet drink. Meetings with Michael Grade and the possibility of an audition at the local Darby and Joan Club are directed at the already pummelled ear of the hapless artiste as a feeling of acute aggression begins to grow in his already battered and abused body. The once relaxed smile suddenly lapses into a fixed leer as the bullshitter (see Bullshitting) rambles on and on. The more experienced professional will make some excuse regarding a weak bladder and slink off into the night, but a lesser mortal will remain to suffer the torment.

The do-gooder tends to frequent public houses and other licensed premises, so it is often advisable to remain teetotal.

DOUCHE-BAG   A description popularised by a character called Magnet (who shall remain nameless), and must be filed alongside Pooh-bum, Groupie, etc.

DRESSING ROOMS   Variable, depending on the status of the act. Completely unknown semi-professional (and sometimes professional) bands might find themselves changing in their van as some promoters regard dressing rooms as places used only by ballet companies and Frank Sinatra. At the other end of the scale a top headline act can expect a large heated area with a sumptuous spread of gastronomic delights which are, incidentally, rarely touched by the performers who are usually too nervous to eat before a show. Thus, many roadies become extremely overweight and have a tendency to drink far too many of the leftovers.

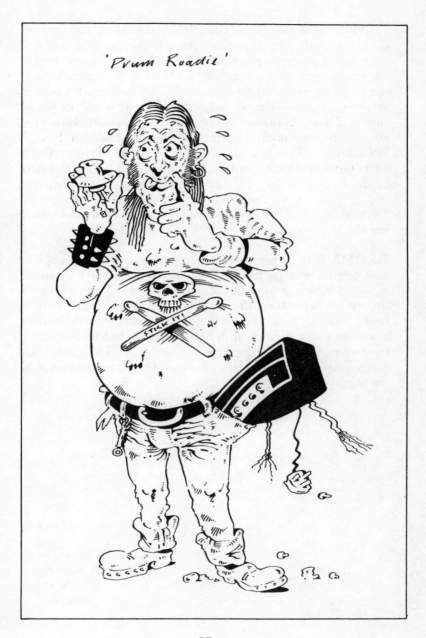

'Drum Roadie'

Outdoor rock festivals tend to have the Portacabin type of dressing room. This is probably due to the fact that very few large fields possess a permanent dressing room. These portable changing rooms are usually quite effective from a practical point of view, but do seem to have a habit of attracting strange drunkards who help themselves to the resident liquor. These characters are rarely ejected as everybody presumes that they must be friends of one of the others.

Classic example of a dressing room is at the Marquee Club in London, which resembles the inside of a huge graffitied coffin.

DRUM ROADIE A person who is no good at twiddling knobs.

DRUMMER A person who hits things (including people), and often develops piles. He is usually the least sensitive member in any group and tends to prefer the physical security of his drum kit to the namby-pamby meanderings of the more, shall we say, perceptive type. Drummers like to experiment with a variety of different things including footwear, explosives, alcohol, drugs, and hairstyles. They also like staying up late in order to put some of these experiments to the test.

EARLY NIGHT   This is an exercise in wishful thinking, often thought about but rarely put into practice on tour. This is due largely to the fact that last night's hangover, so predominant before the show, is now taking second place to an adrenalin-induced state of contentment. The original fear of 'Can I get through the gig?' has been replaced by an attitude of 'Can I get through the next four hours and join the dawn patrol (see Dawn Patrol) for a final celebration of yet another successful concert?'

The answer is, in most cases, summed up by one small word: yes.

Classic quote: 'There's nothing like an early night, and this is nothing like an early night!'

EGO   Self-esteem. Individuality. A feeling of self-motivated confidence.

EGO-TRIPPER   A self-esteemed individually big-headed prick.

ENCORE   Encores have been around since Adam and Eve, and although the original meaning was a 'request on demand', the demands are now requested for a multitude of reasons, for example:

(1) My bus doesn't go for twenty-five minutes and it's cold outside.

(2) The bird I've pulled likes the band and she wants to stay.

(3) I'm the tour manager and you've only played for fifty-five minutes, and unless you play the full hour, as per contract, we won't get paid.

(4) We really did enjoy the band and would honestly like to hear some more.

'We were playing at an open air pop festival in Belgium. Our contract stated that a Leslie 145 speaker was to be provided for the Manfred organ, but when we arrived we found that the promoter had provided the wrong type of speaker. The band refused to appear until a Leslie was found. The promoter didn't know much about musical equipment but he rushed off to see if he could find us what we wanted. Twenty minutes later a pleased promoter reappeared, announcing that he'd found a Leslie. When asked where it was, he pointed to a girl standing beside him: "Manfred Mann, this is Leslie."'

MANFRED MANN

EUROPEAN TOUR   A huge undertaking considering the amount of major cities and towns available, but made less so by the political structure of the Warsaw Pact.

After the United States and Japan, West Germany offers the greatest potential to professional gigging and recording artistes, both in sales and venues available. Its historical standing as the springboard to success of many of the sixties stars is well known and must be respected.

Holland is well known for its cultural attitude. Belgium isn't. Scandinavia has a small but enthusiastic population of music followers, while Italy has a small anarchic fringe who tend to use the rock concert as an excuse to publicize some political issue, though not always. France is normally construed as Paris.

In the past, bands have ventured to Iron Curtain countries but because of their economic climate have returned home laden with furs, cut glass and wooden carvings but

41

minus their Levis, fountain pens, records, etc.

Great Britain is part of Europe, but the British tour is an entity in itself (see British Tour), and offers many practical advantages such as language, lifestyle, currency etc. This assumes, of course, that the individuals are British; it probably wouldn't apply to a troupe of Lithuanian nose flautists.

EXTRAS Those 'extra' sums of money demanded by receptionists when checking out of hotels, which are usually greeted with gasps of disbelief and mass swoonings.

It is very easy to spend a vast amount of money without moving from your room, especially if the hotel is above three-star status. Room service, drinks and, above all, telephone calls can amount to a staggering total. That genial gesture in the bar at 2 a.m. could set you back a good £25.00, but who cares when you're having fun? You do, eight hours later.

Why, you may ask, do people spend so much money in hotels?

Boredom, mate, bloody boredom.

Then why not go out and find somewhere cheaper?

Because you've been doing that all around the world for the last nine months and that's become bloody boring too! Well . . . maybe.

FEARGAL Word invented by Quo's Rick Parfitt meaning chips, as in "I could go a nice Feargal butty" (a chip sandwich). Comes from Feargal Sharkey – Sharkey – darkie – darkie's lips – chips.

FILOFAX A pocket appointments/diary/address book distinguishable from the others because it has inserts to make up your very own combinations of practically anything. Pick and mix music papers, maps, addresses, diaries etc.

The Filofax features in this book because of its unbelievable rise in popularity in the music/show business area and, it seems, right across the board of people with a lot of money to spend on keeping their personal facts and info close by at all times.

Filofax was until recently used chiefly by clergymen and the army and was probably invented by a Canadian at the beginning of the century.

They are now fast becoming status symbols with their leather binders which can easily cost several hundred pounds, and are much favoured by Sloane Rangers, film stars, rock stars, and others.

More often than not Filofaxes don't quite fit into a jacket pocket or discreetly into a handbag so they have to be carried in the hand, which is fine if you are sitting alone in your own toilet in your own home, but problems can and do arise in a busy nightclub or pub or in the back of a cab when you need to put it down for a few moments. So, after weeks, months or years of collating facts, figures, phone numbers, photos and personal essentials with practically no effort at all, you can achieve that feeling of having the bottom of your world fall out as your brain calculates the problems of losing so much to so many.

It has been estimated that if Rod Stewart, Vivien Ventura, John McEnroe and Lord Lichfield all lost their Filofaxes at the same party, within forty-eight hours the whole of society and show business would know exactly what each of them was doing and who they had done it with.

FIVE-K RIG A PA system (see PA System) recommended by sound companies to mullahs for calling the faithful to prayer. NB: Five-k means 5,000 watts (quite loud).

FLIGHT CASE Long gone are the days when all the separate pieces of equipment were thrown totally unprotected into the back of the van to rattle around and get damaged as it sped at ninety miles an hour along a bumpy 'B' road. Today we have the luxury of the flight case built as solid as a brick shit-house and weighing just as much. Often costing as much as and sometimes more than what it actually contains, it does in the long run save the owner money and the inconvenience of replacing vital equipment.

FLOAT Petty cash for dirty deeds (see Xs).

FLOAT A LOG (see also Strangle a Darkie) Going to the toilet and doing biggies, as in 'I knew I shouldn't have had that Indian last night. You should have seen the log I floated this morning.'

Logs are 'sent to the coast' when the loo is flushed.

FOREIGN RECORD COMPANY MEALS Where the Managing Director spends all evening talking to the singer, and the A and R man keeps asking the guitarist if he's a roadie. This of course is only if the band in question is selling a significant number of records. If not, the foreign record

'Drumstick Flightcase'

company meal will not materialize, only a foreign hamburger-stand selling foreign hamburgers to foreigners.

FORMING A BAND   Probably the most artistic form of sadomasochism in existence. A most dangerous exercise that can lead to broken friendships, broken noses, and mild schizophrenia. Frustration, depression, and euphoria mingle under a haze of acute insecurity. The phrase 'Don't worry, in a couple of weeks' time we'll all look back at this moment and laugh' repeats itself with alarming regularity, but at the end of the day it's still more fun than clocking on at the factory, and any band that survives this ordeal finally to tour and make records deserves all the success in the world.

GAFFA TAPE A form of adhesive tape invented for roadies (see Back Line) and rowdies (see Air Hostess). A chemically woven alternative to Superglue. It tends to turn up in the most unusual places at the most undesired moments, e.g. on the soles of the shoes when one is sitting cross-legged amongst the most exclusive company.

It is usually found plastered across stages, multicore cables, guitar leads, guitarists, drummers' trousers, and unwelcome guests. Colours vary between grey and grey.

GIGS Bookings, engagements, etc. It really doesn't matter if it's the Wheatly Hill Disabled Soldiers and Sailors Club (yes, it really did exist, probably still does) or the Wembley Arena, because as far as the travelling musician or roadie is concerned a gig is a gig (is a gig).

The derivation of the actual word seems to be shrouded in mystery. Some say it's an abbreviation of the statement 'God, it's gross!' – a statement, we might hasten to add, made every day of the year the world over by men of the road on entering an establishment of somewhat debatable allure. This etymology is highly probable unless one works in upper-class regions of California. In this case the phrase 'Gee, it's great!' would probably apply.

'I was playing with the Roulettes and we were offered a gig in Manchester on New Year's Eve 1966. We didn't really

47

want to play on New Year's Eve but we decided to go because we needed the money.

We had a 15 cwt van which didn't have a heater. It was very cold and I can remember icicles hanging inside the van. On the way the van began to boil and eventually broke down. Luckily our road manager was a part-time mechanic and managed to get it going. Five miles on we had a puncture and began to feel doomy as we had 100 miles to go in the last hour.

We eventually arrived (a few hours late). I can't remember the name of the street but the number was 66-70. All we found was a pile of rubble which hadn't been a club for a long time. Someone was obviously having a joke.

We had to decide whether to go back to London or stay in Manchester for the night. As it was 9.30 by now we decided to stay and managed to find a boarding house. Our landlady was a jovial thing who, on hearing our story of woe, said, "Never mind, kids, have a New Year drink" – and proceeded to pour liberal helpings of whisky into half-pint mugs.

Next morning as we sat at the breakfast table with terrible hangovers she presented us with the bill for the rooms – and the drinks.

I've never worked on New Year's Eve since.'

RUSS BALLARD

GIG WAGONS In formative days vans, but nowadays limousines or at least Ford Granadas.

GOING THROUGH THE MOTIONS An inevitable predicament that most established bands find themselves in when they've been playing the same set night after night, week after week, month after month and, quite often, year after year.

A good, professional and presentable show is the ultimate goal of any serious act, but once this pinnacle of perfection is soul-searchingly achieved, that much-abused state, 'boredom', is often arrived at.

'Gig Wagon'

This state of boredom can be overcome, perhaps, by individual members indulging more and more in what could be loosely described as 'wine, women and song' (and not necessarily in that order). Unfortunately, if the individuals in question are not of the same mind, this alternative might not be effective.

In these circumstances desperate measures such as chinning (see Chinning) the lead guitarist in front of 3,000 fans might be employed. If this method does not succeed, then a 'back to the drawing board' attitude could be advisable.

GROOVE   A rhythmic flow created by a member of a band in order to inspire other, less creative, personnel. A small bloodstained furrow bestowed upon said member's cranium if he doesn't.

GROUPIES   'A complete fallacy, darlin'.'

'I remember everyone around the Beatles had a terrible job convincing anybody in authority that they had any right to be there or were in fact in the Beatles party. We printed up all kinds of very elaborate identification cards and press passes and goodness knows what for each and every tour

but they didn't work in most places because even if the promoter or the hotel manager had got it it didn't really get down to the guy on the hotel door. I always remember one particular occasion in a Texas hotel where apart from the Beatles themselves most of the rest of us just couldn't get into that hotel. "Look," they said, "the only people who get in here are people who have got hotel keys." We kept telling them that we'd get hotel keys as soon as they let us through the doors to check in. "Oh no," they said, "you don't get in without a key, fella." End of story.'

TONY BARROW

GUEST LIST   A piece of paper with far too many names on it, usually kept at the stage door. A tour manager's night-mare and often the reason why the band stays out of the way in the dressing room. NB: Tour managers often become very irate on discovering that the names on the list start to vary in handwriting styles and ink colours.

HAPPENING This particular expression has a dual meaning. Firstly, a descriptive term rarely employed nowadays which has its origins in the heady days of the late sixties and meaning, quite simply, an event. The event in question was usually a pop festival, or a culturally-inclined gathering.

Secondly, a compliment, normally followed by the word 'man', as in 'The gig was really happening, man.'

HARP ON To express oneself verbally in a continually tedious fashion, usually to the annoyance of anyone within earshot. Remarks are, more often than not, negative, and are nearly always issued by a whinger (see Whinge).

HARRY Slang for flash. Harry Dash – flash.

HAUNTINGS Malicious practical jokes administered by mischievous members of rock and roll entourages on more stable personnel at spooky locations. These locations are often ancient chateaux or English castles being used for 'location recordings' (see Location Recordings).

HEADBANGERS Headbangers (see Headbangers).

HEAD JOB American term for fellatio. Often sought after by rock musicians. (The act, not the meaning.)

HIGH TECH A modern term, often used to describe the

'HeadBangers!'

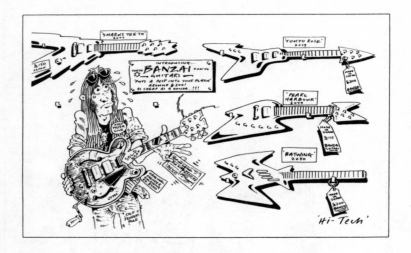

latest batch of Japanese guitars retailing at £215 which send shivers down the spines of vintage guitar collectors who've spent the last fifteen years paying out thousands of pounds on very old instruments with limited technology.

HOs   Hangers-on. Similar in many ways to that well-known species the ligger (see Ligger).

HORRORS   State of panic or unpleasantness often brought on by over-indulgence, or when things get out of control.

There was once a remarkable character in the record industry who still works very successfully in the publishing field and who, ten years ago, was a well-known and respected guitarist.

The original Advision studios used to be in New Bond Street in a basement (since demolished) and the gentleman in question was booked for a session one sunny afternoon.

It was standard procedure for musicians to bring their equipment to the level of the studio by a very antiquated and unreliable lift. The guitarist duly loaded his equip-

ment – amplifier, guitar etc. – and his person into the lift and pressed the button to descend. The lift, with much creaking and complaining, lowered him slowly downwards and stopped eighteen inches short of the studio floor. Every effort by the studio staff to open the collapsible metal door was to no avail and our guitarist friend was well and truly trapped. Being, like most of us, rather prone to claustrophobia, he proceeded to panic with much yelling, shouting and shaking of the metal box. Various telephone calls were made to lift service engineers who, in true English fashion, could not make it for several hours, and the producer, engineer and arranger decided the only way the session could go ahead was if the guitarist actually played in the lift. Microphones, music stands, mike stands, headphones and all the paraphernalia required were collapsed and passed through the gaps in the metal bars to the panicking musician.

Like a true pro the guitarist, with perspiration popping on his forehead and an extremely high adrenalin count, set up his equipment and sat, white-faced, waiting for instructions. The session duly commenced and the gentleman played with his usual flair and imagination, the only difference being that at the end of each take, immediately the last note had died away, he would scream at the top of his voice protests like "Get me the fuck out of here!" and "Where are the bleeding lift engineers?" This would continue until the count-in for the next take, whereupon he would stop his panicking and immediately play.

After three hours the session was complete, and just at that time the lift engineers arrived. As all the other musicians were preparing to leave, the lift man looked through the bars at our friend, inserted a rather odd-shaped key into an equally odd-looking hole, turned it in a rather complicated way and unlocked a little box. Then he pressed a button, whereupon our guitarist friend, dragging microphones, leads, music stands and half a drum kit across the studio floor, sailed upwards out of sight.

MARTIN RUSHENT

57

HOTELS Places where you do things you wouldn't normally do at home.

A hell of a lot of money could be saved on tour if hotels only charged by the amount of hours spent asleep in one's allotted bed. Admittedly hotels would then lose a fortune when a band stayed the night, but just think how much they would make from a convention of travelling Bible salesmen.

Talking of Bibles, many hotels in the Western hemisphere equip their rooms with a copy of Gideon's Bible, a sort of Holiday Inn New Testament. This particular book is no doubt consulted by the average guilt-ridden atheist on retiring, but the regular rock and roll performer regards this publication with a certain amount of disdain (possibly misguided).

Once again, status determines the type of hostel offered to the travelling performer, and this ranges from the self-contained and highly personal (cheap) 'Guest House', to the hugely commercial but often luxurious 'Five-Star Hotel'. 'Getting away with murder' is much more easily managed at the latter, where money talks (in most languages).

Certain mentally obese rock stars have caused damage on a par with that administered by international terrorists, but with that contemporary expression 'American Express?' they have been confronted in a most polite manner with the genial response, 'That'll do nicely, sir.'

HUGHIE/RALPH/BARF/WHARK/EUROPE/CHUNDER (see also Vomit) An internationally known folk song which is recited, without fail, by a nauseated person to the nearest toilet bowl, sink or carpet. The length of the recital varies, depending on circumstances, company, or intake.

HUGLY STICK As in 'been hit with the hugly stick'. An ancient ritual originating in the north-east of England.

HUMILITY An attribute not to be recommended to young people embarking on careers in the entertainment industry. Failure to comply with this advice may result in a sense of failure, or even mental disorder.

59

'Humper'

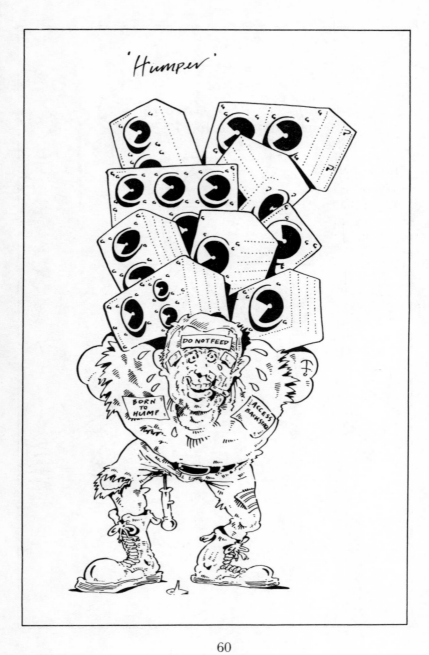

'On the first night of the Sex Pistols' one and only tour of England, after setting up their gear, we were all ready, the band turned up, amps 100 per cent on. All we needed was Johnny Rotten himself. Everyone – roadies, general hangers-on – was wondering what Johnny Rotten would be like. We were also wondering how he would like his mikes, lights etc. The soundcheck was at 4 o'clock in the afternoon, and the show was to go on at 9 p.m. We waited and waited and waited. Where could he be? It was now 8 p.m., and the punters were coming into the theatre, but still no sign of Johnny. Then, all of a sudden, he appeared in the centre of the stage. I shouted from the mixing desk, "How do you want the mikes, John? Treble, bassy, or what?" He looked up to the desk and yelled back, "On, you silly fucker!! On!!" There's a professional, I thought, there's a professional!'

JERRY BAXTER

HUMPER A gentleman of unknown background bred solely for the purpose of carrying all the equipment heavier than a plectrum in and out of the gig (see Gigs). Occasionally one will break out and become an HO (see HOs) until accepted as a roadie (see Crew) who can then stand around and watch the humper. Wages negotiable.

HYPED-UP Being in a state of mental and physical arousal, brought on by any number of dominating factors, e.g. adrenalin, drink, drugs, preconceived thoughts, etc.

IDIOT TEST This nightly ritual is usually bestowed upon the least experienced member of a road crew and basically requires the novice to check the stage and dressing room areas for neglected items. These 'items' could vary from a £6,000 Gibson Les Paul guitar to a bottle of Jack Daniels. The test usually proves to be negative, although smaller 'items' are occasionally found.

IMAGE Any young performer considering a future in show business must be made aware, right from the start, that his personal appearance and individual outlook on life will be kept under the greatest scrutiny and preyed upon by the powers that be.

This professional intrusion into personal life is bad enough when applied to the solo artiste, e.g. Wham(?), Elton John, Howard Jones, Michael Jackson, that little choirboy in that stupid Andrew Lloyd-Webber song etc., but when it involves a whole band, the problems definitely multiply themselves by the number of members, and sometimes more, depending upon individual egos (see Ego).

Each performer's image can fluctuate incredibly in the course of a career (how long is a career? – how long is a piece of string?) It depends really upon the quality of ligging, the strength of one's liver and the ability to say no when what is left of the brain wants to say yes.

There are of course several exceptions to this rule such as genuinely talented performers – the likes of Phil Collins and

'Image'

Eric Clapton immediately spring to mind – who can transcend all temporary musical vogues by simply being themselves. Their images stand in their own shadows and without doubt take second place to an honest and natural ability. Years of physical and mental abuse, coupled with the ageing process of every normal human being, and double coupled with the premature paranoia of every image-conscious rock veteran, will inevitably lead to a state of narcissistic panic.

Telltale signs of being out of condition, out of shape and out to lunch are when the make-up girl at *Top of the Pops* bypasses the make-up tray and reaches for the packet of Polyfilla reserved for such occasions.

In response to numerous requests from the aforementioned Dorian Gray-ites there is soon to be a book published by the unknown Welsh keep-fit fanatic Wayne Rhonda entitled *How To Stay Unknown and Keep Fit*. At no great expense the authors have managed to extract excerpts from the unknown Wayne's publication whilst interviewing him under the table at the Swansea and District picket line training club:

'*The Alarm Clock Technique* Depending upon which side of the bed you sleep, this is very good for the exercise of one arm. On hearing the alarm clock ringing in the morning, the subject is required to thrust the arm out through 90 degrees in the general direction of the wife, mistress, girlfriend, boyfriend, sheep etc., and with the combined usage of the vocal chords (see Vocal Chord Exercise) establish the need for silence by reciting the relevant verse from Rhonda's book of unknown poems:

> *As morning breaks and wind does too,*
> *My head doth ache here next to you.*
> *That clock that rings, please turn it off,*
> *Then get downstairs and make the tea.*

'*Bar Exercises* Being generous can keep you fit. Remember, the more rounds you buy the more times you have to walk to the bar; this keeps the blood circulating and develops leg muscles. Be warned, though, that in clubs where waitress service is compulsory this exercise should be

'Bar Exercises'
For
Beerdrinkers an' Hellraisers!

avoided although it can be substituted with the consumption of vast amounts of lager and real ale (see RAF), thus necessitating the need to walk/run/stagger towards the nearest toilet (and occasionally back).

'*General Exercises for Fingers, Neck and Feet*   Best practised after midnight in any discotheque. On hearing a suitably rythmic piece of music the subject should click the fingers, nod the head or tap the feet. Experienced Rhonda fanatics will, with practice and determination, find themselves eventually able to execute all three exercises simultaneously, thus being only one step away from "The Big Move".

'*The Big Move*   Otherwise known as "making a right twat of yourself on the dance floor". This exercise in uninhibited gyrations is particularly good for the stomach muscles which are used extensively while throwing up over your partner.'

As the chairman of the bloozervative party, Rick Parfitt, humbly said during his recent dinner speech on the subject 'The Importance of Being Ernest Image', 'One must have moderation, but plenty of it.'

'I'M FINE REALLY'   A universal expression, but in the context of this book used only by band members found prostrate over the dressing room toilet.

IMPOSSIBLE DREAM   Scoring in Finland.

'In 1970 I worked for a short time for a studio called Command, which was a big place – three studios, big cutting room, copying suites etc. Two years before that it was looked on as something special, but by the time I got there it was going broke, and in fact it did eventually go broke. One day all the engineers were told that there were going to be some cutbacks made to save the place. One of the cutbacks was that the cheese and tomato sandwiches in the staff canteen wouldn't have any tomato in them.'

VIC MAILE

INDIAN RESTAURANTS   Very popular with touring musicians and road crews, probably because they are usually the only eating houses still open after a gig.

Dining at one of these restaurants can sometimes prove to be rather traumatic, inasmuch as there is the constant worry regarding one's digestive system and the possible threat of violence from the table full of drunken lorry drivers behind you. But the main threat comes from the establishment's sound system.

67

The initial idea to play soft, conducive Indian folk music quietly in the background was commendable enough, but of late the choice of material seems to have swung to a sort of manic Hindu disco. Saturday night Sikh fever. The quality has slipped a bit too. The ethnic recordings by Ravi Shankar have now been replaced by some out-of-work abattoir attendant from Leeds, whose sitar-playing leaves everything to the imagination.

The above account may not be altogether true, of course. The abattoir attendant may actually come from Bradford.

INVITING A FRIEND UP ON STAGE FOR A JAM A drastic mistake. Musicians when appearing professionally tend on the whole to keep their level of intoxication down to a sensible level. Musicians' friends masquerading as a part of the audience don't. As a result, a request from the band on stage (more often than not shared with the audience) can lead to a state of panic in the innocent musical bystander who suddenly realizes that he's totally incapable of focusing on an instrument, let alone playing it.

There are, in the authors' experience, two basic methods of dealing with this situation. (1) Immediately assume an inane and fixed grin whilst walking in an incredibly cool fashion in the general direction of the stage (unfortunately this is almost impossible when pissed). If by chance the destination aimed for is reached, it is usually wise, if handed an instrument, to keep the volume control set to zero. (2) Run.

ITINERARY According to the *Collins English Dictionary* an itinerary is 'a record of travel; a plan or line of travel; a route; a guidebook for travellers'. According to *The Language of Rock 'n' Roll* it can be anything from that down to a garbled secondhand message over the telephone at 2.30 a.m. saying approximately where and when the musician/performer is supposed to be for the last-minute gig just in for the following day.

Itineraries are as old as touring itself, but over the years, as the distances between gigs has increased, the time between

'Impossible Dream...

...Scoring in Finland'

them become shorter, the equipment and staging more complex, and the entourage bigger, they have become as important a piece of equipment as, say, an amplifier or guitar. What's the use of having the best band, crew and equipment in the world if none of it knows where it's going?

Comprehensive, around-the-clock information is essential to any tour, and the itinerary is the Bible of the road, there to be consulted daily to provide each individual member of the entourage with the necessary details to go about his business with the minimum of delay and inconvenience. Theoretically speaking, that is. In practice every tour can guarantee at least one casualty (see Casualty). It's true to say that generally speaking fifty per cent of the people on tour at eight o'clock in the morning can't find their itinerary let alone find the page relating to that particular day and on top of all that read the name of the next city. The sight of forty grown children being herded through an airport terminal with eight hours' sleep between them is not for the squeamish.

The Japanese are the epitome of precision when it comes to itineraries. On arrival (following the customary bowing etc.) every member of the tour is given one (an itinerary, that is) which lists in unbelievable detail all the daily movements. Everything is timed to the minute and strictly adhered to. In Spain, on the other hand, everything is organised to the nearest half day.

The tour manager (see Tour Manager) usually has the responsibility of putting the itinerary together and at the top level it can take months of preparation to iron out the minutest of potential problems.

The following is a perfect example of what a heavy itinerary is all about. It was put together for Phil Collins by Andy Mackrill, arguably one of the most respected tour managers in the business.

Phil Collins and his Hot Tub Club.

the 'No Jacket Required' tour 1985

February

10	Sun	(Set-Up)	Nottingham
11	Mon	Royal Centre	Nottingham
12	Tue	Apollo Theatre	Manchester
13	Wed	Apollo Theatre	Glasgow
14	Thu	Off	
15	Fri	City Hall	Newcastle
16	Sat	City Hall	Sheffield
17	Sun	Royal Albert Hall	London
18	Mon	Royal Albert Hall	London
19	Tue	Royal Albert Hall	London
20	Wed	Royal Albert Hall	London
21	Thu	Royal Albert Hall	London
22	Fri	Royal Albert Hall	London
23	Sat	International Arena, NEC	Birmingham
24	Sun	Off	
25	Mon	Philipshalle	Dusseldorf
26	Tue	Forest National	Brussels
27	Wed	Ahoy Sportpaleis	Rotterdam
28	Thu	Off	

March

01	Fri	Scandanavium	Am Zoon · Seinf.	Gothenberg
02	Sat	Isstadion		Stockholm
03	Sun	Valbyhallen		Copenhagen
04	Mon	Stadhalle		Bremen
05	Tue	Off		
06	Wed	Omnisports-Bercy		Paris
07	Thu	Festhalle		Frankfurt
08	Fri	Rudy Sedlmayer Halle		Munich
09	Sat	Off		
10	Sun	Hallenstadion		Zurich
11	Mon	Sporthalle Boeblingen		Stuttgart
12	Tue	Off		
13	Wed	Salle de la Beaujoire		Nantes
14	Thu	Patinoire de Meriadec		Bordeaux
15	Fri	Palais Des Sports		Toulouse
16	Sat	Espace Tony Garnier		Lyon
17	Sun	Halle 7 - Palais Des Beaulieu		Lausanne
18	Mon	Off - Return to London		

March

25	Mon	Leave London for Australia	
26	Tue		
27	Wed	Arrive Australia	
28	Thu	Off	
29	Fri	Festival Hall	Brisbane **
30	Sat	Festival Hall	Brisbane
31	Sun	Festival Hall	Brisbane

April

01	Mon	Off	
02	Tue	Off	
03	Wed	Entertainment Centre	Sydney
04	Thu	Entertainment Centre	Sydney
05	Fri	Off	
06	Sat	Opera House	Sydney
07	Sun	Opera House	Sydney
08	Mon	Off	
09	Tue	Entertainment Centre	Sydney
10	Wed	Entertainment Centre	Sydney **
11	Thu	Off	
12	Fri	Sports & Entertainment Centre	Melbourne
13	Sat	Sports & Entertainment Centre	Melbourne
14	Sun	Sports & Entertainment Centre	Melbourne
15	Mon	Sports & Entertainment Centre	Melbourne **
16	Tue	Off	
17	Wed	Memorial Drive Tennis Centre	Adelaide
18	Thu	Off	
19	Fri	Entertainment Centre	Perth **
20	Sat	Entertainment Centre	Perth
21	Sun	Leave for Japan	
22	Mon	Arrive Japan	
23	Tue	Nippon Budokan	Tokyo
24	Wed	Off	
25	Thu	Fukuoka Sun Palace Hall	Fukuoka
26	Fri	Osaka Festival-Hall	Osaka
27	Sat	Nagoya Shi Kokaido	Nagoya
28	Sun	Off in Tokyo	
29	Mon	Leave Japan , Arrive USA same day - Gain one day by crossing International Dateline	

** These dates in Australia are options and will be
confirmed or cancelled in due course.

May

10	Fri	The Centrum (Set-Up)	Worcester, MA
11	Sat	The Centrum (Set-Up)	Worcester, MA
12	Sun	The Centrum (Show)	Worcester, MA
13	Mon	The Forum	Montreal, Canada
14	Tue	Off	
15	Wed	Radio City Music Hall	New York, NY
16	Thu	Radio City Music Hall	New York, NY
17	Fri	Radio City Music Hall	New York, NY
18	Sat	The Spectrum	Philadelphia, PA
19	Sun	Off	
20	Mon	The Spectrum	Philadelphia, PA
21	Tue	Hampton Coliseum	Hampton, VA
22	Wed	Coliseum	Greensboro, NC
23	Thu	The Omni	Atlanta, GA
24	Fri	Jefferson Coliseum	Birmingham, AL
25	Sat	Mid-South Coliseum	Memphis, TN
26	Sun	Off	
27	Mon	The Summit	Houston, TX
28	Tue	The Summit	Houston, TX
29	Wed	Reunion Arena	Dallas, TX
30	Thu	Reunion Arena	Dallas, TX
31	Fri	Off	

June

01	Sat	Compton Terrace	Chandler, AZ
02	Sun	Irvine Meadows	Laguna Hills, CA
03	Mon	Irvine Meadows	Laguna Hills, CA
04	Tue	Universal Amphitheatre	Universal City, CA
05	Wed	Universal Amphitheatre	Universal City, CA
06	Thu	Universal Amphitehatre	Universal City, CA
07	Fri	Coliseum	Oakland, CA
08	Sat	Coliseum	Oakland, CA
09	Sun	Coliseum	Oakland, CA
10	Mon	Off	
11	Tue	Cal Expo Amphitheatre	Sacramento, CA
12	Wed	Off	
13	Thu	McNichols Arena	Denver, CO
14	Fri	Off	
15	Sat	Kemper Arena	Kansas City, MO
16	Sun	Kiel Auditorium	St. Louis, MO
17	Mon	Poplar Creek	Hoffman Estates, IL
18	Tue	Poplar Creek	Hoffman Estates, IL
19	Wed	Rupp Arena	Lexington, KY
20	Thu	Off	
21	Fri	Merriweather Post	Columbia, MD
22	Sat	Civic Center	Hartford, CT
23	Sun	Performing Arts Center	Saratoga Springs, NY
24	Mon	Off	

73

June

25	Tue	Richfield Coliseum	Cleveland, OH
26	Wed	Richfield Coliseum	Cleveland, OH
27	Thu	Pine Knob Music Theatre	Clarkston, MI
28	Fri	Pine Knob Music Theatre	Clarkston, MI
29	Sat	CNE Stadium	Toronto, Canada
30	Sun	Off	

July

| 01 | Mon | Madison Square Garden | New York, NY |
| 02 | Tue | Madison Square Garden | New York, NY |

JUST A FEW SIMPLE POINTS THAT EVERYONE SHOULD TAKE NOTE OF.

1.   TELEPHONE Numbers contained in this intinerary were
believed to be correct at the time it was prepared. They
are however, subject to change and/or could be supplemented
at a later date.

2.   LAMINATED PASSES will be issued to everyone working on
the tour. These passes are for your OWN use only and should
not be given away to anyone for the purpose of gaining
access to a venue or a backstage area. All passes will be
named or numbered and our security people will be watching
for anyone wearing a laminated pass who is unknown to them.
Such people will be stopped on sight and if it is discovered
that they have been given the pass by one of you, it will be
taken off them and they will be escorted out of the
backstage area and building. The numbering or name system
will then indicate where the pass came from. Stick-on passes
are to be used for guests.

3.   GUEST TICKETS will be available at each venue, but only
in a limited quantity. The availability will obviously be
very limited in cities like London, New York and Los
Angeles. I will operate on a first come-first served basis
and I will try to be fair to everyone along the way. However
once the allocation has been used up, That is the end of
that. Please note that in the majority of venues on the tour
guests must have a ticket as well as a pass in order to gain
access to the venue seating areas. GUESTS ARE NOT ALLOWED IN
EITHER THE STAGE OR BACKSTAGE AREAS FROM THIRTY MINUTES
PRIOR TO THE SHOW, DURING THE SHOW AND TILL THIRTY MINUTES
AFTER THE SHOW ENDS.

4.   HOTELS Please make sure you pay your hotel extras/
incidentals upon your departure from hotels. If you are sure
you have no charges, could you please still stop by the
reception desk and formally check out. This will hopefully
save any arguments later. It also stops the hotels from
trying to charge for an extra night because you have not
technically checked out. If you ever have any problems with
hotels along the tour TELL ME !

5.   HOT MEALS AT SHOWS and food and drink in general,
are provided for people working on the tour only. It is not
a restuarant/bar service for guests.

Thanks
ANDY MACKRILL

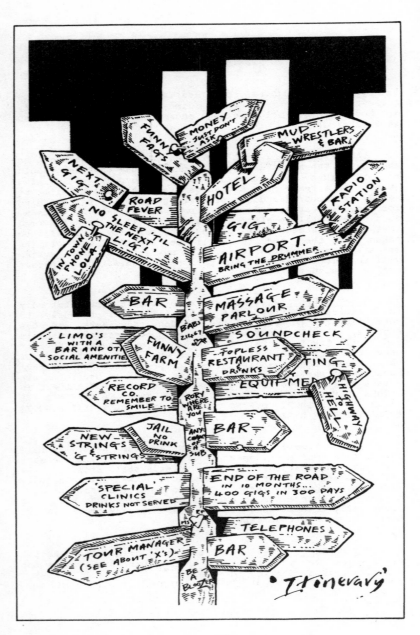

JAILBAIT   A young lady who though physically and visually in a definate state of sexual arousal is definately below the age of consent and must be avoided, especially in Iron Curtain countries.

JAMES BOND SYNDROME   A cruel, yet briefly humorous experience involving a team of musicians and some unsuspecting young waiter or other subservient type. Having been spotted by a team of eagle-eyed piss-takers, the humble novice need make only one mistake to hear the well-rehearsed but raucus rendition of the James Bond theme tune.

The more hearty versions are usually reserved for the more humiliating cock-ups, e.g. the dropping of large trays of drinks or food, or the completely unforgivable burning of somebody's moustache with a well-meant but unexpectedly large-flamed cigarette lighter.

JAPAN   See under most letters.

JAPANESE HOSPITALITY   Very favourable, especially if one is a visiting Western musician, or Western anything.

JAPANESE TOURS   A form of mental torture organised by sadistic agents in which 12–15 grown men endure a gruelling flight, suffer jet lag, food poisoning, dysentery, maintenance orders, Japanese vodka, raw fish, baths designed for circus midgets, roaming herds of flashing cameras, more of everything again, and then have to get used to English tea again.

JINGLES   The often mindless musical meanderings sometimes associated with TV and radio adverts.

JOBSWORTH   Derived from the classic quote 'It's more than me job's worth'. The disciple of discipline is usually of military extraction and prefers to work in uniform, i.e. cinema commissionaire, hotel night porter (a dying breed, thank heaven; see Night Porter), and British Rail employees.

In the musical context he belongs to a passing era but pops up occasionally at some out-of-the-way village hall dance, with strict orders to close up the premises within minutes of the band's last tune.

This can of course pose many a problem, especially if the innocent combo possesses too much sound equipment.

That plaintive yet despotic request to 'get that bloody lot out of here within five minutes, or it'll be more than me job's worth' has destroyed many a naive young artiste's confidence. Yet those who are long in the tooth know that this yeoman of traditional good will can prove, somewhat paradoxically, to be a person of immense character.

There is a tale from yesteryear which relates the experiences of one such 'jobsworth', and it goes something like this:

Jobsworth   'We've 'ad 'em all 'ere y'know, why, only last week we 'ad that famous jazz player, Duke of Wellington (Duke Ellington). They were bloody skint, 'is band!'

Musicians   'How do you know that?'

Jobsworth   'Well, they were so bloody poor they all sat round a table and shared the same cigarette.'

'We used to truck up and down the country doing gigs and things and on one occasion I arrived at this venue in Huddersfield in my jeans and plimsolls. I went to the door of the club – it was one of those big, heavy doors with a peephole so the security people can check you out – and knocked.

'Japanese Tours'

"Can I come in?" I said.

"No," said the guy on the other side, "you can't come in with jeans and gym shoes on, mate."

"But I'm working here tonight," I said.

"I'm sorry, mate," he said, "you're not coming in with jeans and gym shoes on, no way. Over-eighteens have to wear a tie and jacket."

So I said, "Well, actually I'm Peter Powell."

"You're not Peter Powell," he said. "I've had a hundred and fifty Peter Powells trying to get through this club door and you're not coming in. If you don't go away I'm going to come outside and thump you."

So I went back to the car and put on my stage gear – my Radio One jacket which has all the colours and my name across the front – and went to the door again. The guy opened the peephole thing and I said, "Now do you believe me?"

"Look, mate," he said, "if you keep bothering me like this I'm going to take you down to the nearest police station for causing an obstruction to the door."

I finished up going to the police station myself and rang the club manager from there to explain what was going on. When I arrived back at the club the manager vouched that

I was Peter Powell. The doorman couldn't take it. "I don't believe it," he said, and resigned on the spot.'

PETER POWELL

JOHNNYS An ancient word for contraceptives rarely used these days (the word as well as the contraceptives) because most 'pulls' are on the pill.

JOINTS Cannabis cigarettes (see Wonga). In the sixties and seventies the smoking of joints was a common occurrence at people's pads (flats) and rock events, but with the advent of punk rock in the late seventies it gave way to the alcohol-influenced state of anarchic protest. Still popular with the old hippies.

K   1,000 watts

K x 2   2,000 watts

K x 10   Bloody loud. (NB: Quo at Milton Keynes used a massive 250K PA system.)

KING   By some strange coincidental quirk, three of the most original and influential guitar players of modern times have shared the same surname: B.B. and Albert are Mississippi-bred and apparently related, whereas Freddie was Texas-bred (he is now deceased).
    B.B. King is probably the most respected and best known of the three, and started his career in the late forties, inspired originally by Django Reinhardt and T-Bone Walker. Albert and Freddie appeared on the scene a little later, and like B.B. owe much of their success to the white admirers of the late sixties. Recently a pop group called King have gained popularity, but owe nothing to the above mentioned. Damn shame.

KIT   The drum kit.

KNIGHT IN SHINING ARMOUR   Unknown in the rock world, but see Night of Shining Amour.

KNOWING THE RIGHT PEOPLE   Still one of the quick-

'Knowing the RIGHT People'

est and easiest ways to achieve success in the entertainment business, although students of this particular pastime (getting to know the right people) have often been known to lack pride.

'I was in a rather ageing discotheque up in Norwich and the discotheque unit was powering out about a thousand watts. The dressing room was directly behind the disco unit and the biggest problem was trying to do this local radio interview with this guy. We couldn't do it in the dressing room because there was just too much noise so we had to go into the closet, which was actually a portable loo that had been put in there by the club for desperate entertainers who need to relieve themselves before they go on stage – which is very often the case because you get very nervous. Anyway, we bundled into this makeshift loo. We were just about to start the interview when the door opens and a horrified waitress freaks out seeing the star DJ on the loo with a radio interviewer sitting on his lap and a tape recorder in the basin.'

PETER POWELL

LAID BACK   In the musical context a style which origi-
nated in the Midwest or Deep South of the USA some time in
the early seventies. Reasons given were the hot climate, artistic attitude, and rural ambience. In other climates intoxicants tend to be the major influence.

LAP OF THE GODS   Not four superstars running naked
once round a hotel reception as the term might suggest, but
the tour manager's comment to the management and band
after completing the itinerary to theoretical perfection and
setting off on the first day of a tour, as in 'Right chaps, everything's been checked out that can be, so now we're in the lap
of the gods' (not to mention the inconsistent weather, air-
lines, promoters and mental and body conditions ahead).

'On one occasion the guitarist forgot to turn off his echop-
lex machine and as Cliff finished his introduction to a new
number the machine started playing the intro to the last
number. The guitarist, who was never one to stand on
ceremony, calmly said, "Cor, who the fuck's playing that?"
which made the entire band hysterical, it being a gospel
tour.'

GORDON HASKELL

LAUNDRY   Any band that's been on the road for more
than two weeks will start to consider this word and ponder

85

the need to wash their underpants, socks and tee-shirts which have been regularly turned inside out since the end of the last tour.

The majority of travelling performers in the lower income bracket will, through necessity, wash most of their clothes in the sink of their hotel rooms. Any outstanding attire (jeans etc.) will be gathered en masse and taken by a nominee to the nearest launderette.

Once a group of artistes becomes successful, these menial chores are normally handed over to the kind of hotel staff known as 'room service', who are also related to the food-serving type. They will, given twenty-four hours' notice, wash, starch, iron and generally treat your clothes in a royal fashion befitting a king. Sadly, three pairs of worn-out and patched Levi jeans, four tee-shirts, and some frightfully risqué smalls rarely warrant this kind of attention. Anybody who has coughed up £22 for the restoration of the above will, given time, resort to throwing the whole lot into a bathtub of bubbly soap and spending the £22 on a bottle of champagne.

The greatest risk in having one's day-to-day clothing entrusted to the up-market hotel laundry staff is getting it back on time, especially after a rather celebratory night.

It is very easy to forget some of the more laborious facets of life on the road and many a fragile soul has checked out of a hotel forgetting to pick up his laundry. Five hours and 3,000 miles laters he remembers and requests the tour manager (see Tour Manager) to arrange for his precious cargo to be sent on to the next port of call.

The said package duly arrives at a cost of something akin to the annual gross earnings of the chairman of Levi Strauss. This is the main reason why a band should employ someone who is willing to devote his life to calculating the exact location of other people's clothing, otherwise the entertainers in question will eventually turn to religion because, as any monk will tell you, you can only have one filthy habit.

'LEAN ON IT'   A request from the sound man to a some-what timid guitarist whose passive style is being lost in the outfront 'mix' (see Mix).

'Laid Back'

LICKS   An activity often associated with the tongue, but in this context musical riffs or improvisations expressed by players in order to fulfil their artistic longings or, alternatively, to impress others.

LIFT   A means of hotel travel, but mostly a form of dishonest song-writing whereby the musical thief 'lifts' ideas from other people's records and claims them as his/her own.

LIGGER   Similar to the name-dropper (see Name-dropper) but lacking any sort of pride. He (or she) will often weasel its way into the company of rock celebrities with the sole intention of becoming an aquaintance. The ligger will look down upon the 'name-dropper' for the simple reason that he doesn't put his bunny where his mouth is!

LIGHTS   Lighting rig. Lighting is essential to enhance the presentation of any major rock performance. Atmosphere can be created or lost depending upon the ability of the lights operator, who nowadays (along with other crew members) much prefers the title of 'technician'.

Lighting rigs these days range from those that cost hundreds of thousands of pounds down to those that only light up when two sticks of wood are rubbed together.

One of the authors once graced the stage with a band whose lights consisted of two biscuit tins minus lids, which were raised from the floor by broom handles. The fronts of the tins were covered with sheets of red plastic and hid a 100-watt bulb. Two helpers were required to stand either side of the makeshift stage and switch each tin on and off at will. After the first performance with this revelation in lighting design, Will complained of headaches and left the band.

The other author remembers one particular gig in a huge tent in France where the massively expensive rig lighting for Status Quo completely failed after only the second number due to a faulty generator. In order not to disappoint the several thousand punters (and also lose their money) Quo decided to play the rest of the two-hour set lit by only half a dozen torches held by the management, promoter and

roadies. This night more than one pair of wings (see Wings) was awarded.

LIMO A classic form of transport favoured by groups or artistes who are in a position to get their record companies to pay for it. Particularly used for meeting said performers at airports. The bigger the ego, the more limos. Standard and quality of limo and driver extremely variable depending on which country you are in, e.g. America – latest model Cadillac, Spain – 1943 Seat, or if you have the misfortune to play in Leipzig – five push-bikes.

LIONELS Lionel Barts – farts. Sometimes when bands are sitting around in hotel rooms bored and in a childish mood, Lionels can help. Band members will occasionally take part in a creative pastime known as 'making a farts (Lionels) tape'. This involves the use of a portable cassette player, onto which are recorded the flatulent results of too much real ale and/or curry. These windy efforts are then played back through the band's PA at the next soundcheck (see Soundchecks), and are usually greeted with hilarious acclaim by the road crew.

LOCATION RECORDINGS Rock artistes sometimes choose to record their music in an atmosphere of total togetherness that might not always be achieved in a more business-orientated and domestic setting. This attitude is purely personal; many bands conduct their affairs within a purely urban environment with successful results.

Those performers who feel the need to get away from it all often choose some desolate manor house or castle where, with the help of a mobile recording unit, they transfer their performance onto tape.

This communal existence and the need to relax and let off steam has been known to provoke certain impish characters to take advantage of the rather spookish ambience to reduce the more sensitive co-inhabitants to states of nervous fatigue.

A local pub, normally the one with the easy-going yet financially shrewd landlord, is often regarded as an alterna-

'Limo'

tive communal setting and is increasingly frequented as the recording reaches the laborious stages often associated with overdubs, vocals, rough mixes etc. These landlords, used to earning a paltry living from a few locals, have sometimes been known to fly off to a sunshine holiday on the profits from such an eccentric bunch of steady drinkers.

Location recording is an experience guaranteed to bring out the individuality of the various characters in the set-up.

LOOKALIKES In layman's terms this would be construed as meaning somebody or bodies who bore a passing resemblance to someone else, notably a celebrity or close personal friend of the participants involved.

In rock and roll terms it has evolved into an obsession equalled only by the self-confessed whims of a terminal neurotic.

Points on a scale of one to ten are asked for and will sometimes be awarded for the sheer outrageous level of suggestion, e.g. 'How about nine for Louis Armstrong over there?' when it would have been better to go for three on Marylin Monroe.

For a good contest why not try sending a coach party to the pub round the corner from Fastbuck Recording Studios in Chiswick where in one evening the authors spotted Lassie, three Field Marshal Montgomerys, Lord Lucan, Spit the dog, Anthony Hopkins, Arthur Scargill drinking with Mick McGahey, Chris Bonnington, Art Garfunkel, Geoff Capes, Denis Healey and Elsie Tanner, making a grand total of 118 points in one sitting.

The intrepid participant who submits a polaroid photo (see Polaroid Cameras) of a lookalike will be given a large drink of his choice in lieu of artistic acclaim.

LOVELY MAN A term used more and more these days, particularly in rural areas of England, by fading rock stars to describe the character of his friend, another fading rock star, who is, at that particular moment, throwing up over the microwave.

92

'A couple of years back Jimmy Savile and I were presenting the Christmas *Top of the Pops* show. The cast were assembled, the camera crew were all set up and ready to go, and on came the smoked turkey which had kindly been provided by Harrods. It was set on a table in front of Jimmy and me. The show was half way through when the producer said, "Okay, folks, we'll start cutting up the turkey now to make it look as though we've been gobbling it through the show." My link was coming up and I had to take a leg off the turkey and start to eat it at the same time as introduce the next artiste. Jimmy Savile gave me my cue, I said, "Thanks, Jimmy," leant forward and took hold of the leg, but it was still attached to the turkey. So there I was in front of the cameras, my hand tugging at this turkey leg. "We seem to have a tough old bird here," I said, "I'm trying to pull its leg off," tug, tug, "Oh, it's coming. It's coming, it's coming. . ." I turned to look at the camera ". . . and so is Randy Crawford." Great introduction!'

PETER POWELL

93

MAKE-UP ARTIST   Only in recent years has the make-up artist become a part of many a major act entourage. The overnight superstar in particular loves the excessive use of make-up, which gives him a feeling of, at last, really being in show business.

For television and video shoots make-up is, of course, essential, but for the average rock star sweating under thousands of watts of stage lighting, the MUA is more often than not an unnecessary luxury. She/he is likely to find the job more secure if capable of supplying the artiste with a reasonable massage (see Massage).

MASSAGE   In the *Collins English Dictionary* the word shortly after Massage is Massé, and it explains that in billiards this is a stroke made with the cue held perpendicular, or nearly so. In the language of rock and roll this is probably nearer to the true meaning of the word massage.

A good massage cuts across all language barriers. Grunt, mmmm, oh, ahh, oooo, OK is quite universal. From Basingstoke to Bangkok, from Tolouse to Tokyo a massage is always available and in show business is one of the many luxuries offered by the eager-to-please local promoter.

In Japan a visit to a bath house is a must for every visiting rock and roller. As opposed to some of the seedier joints of say Hamburg or San Francisco, in Tokyo one doesn't immediately think of coming and going, but more of enjoying the total experience. Instead of 'Guttn abent. Gessen

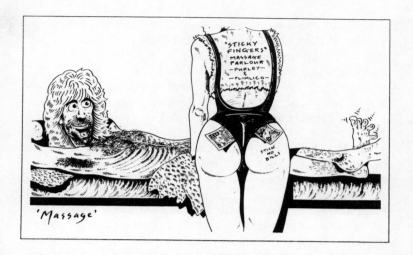

'Massage'

immhere und vipp dem strides off' you will get a courteous
bow and gentle 'Harrow mister. You forrow me and come
lemove nice pants this way cooky baby'.

Rick Parfitt, who will remain nameless, on entering his
private bathroom with a tasty little nip who looked like she
knew how to do a good w. . . ., sorry, with his masseuse, had
the unfortunate experience of slipping on a bar of soap as he
ran across the delicate little bridge which went over the gentle flowing stream which passed through the perfumed room.
Luckily he only killed four precious oriental goldfish as his
arse hit the water. As for the rest of Status Quo, they all
agreed it was a relief to get in there.

MERCHANDISING Swag – big business, provided the
company is working for a popular act. Gone are the days of
the concert programme and the occasional rosette. Nowadays it's the official souvenir programme, official scarf, official sew-on badge, official pin-on badge, official aerobic
headband, official jogging suit, official nuclear fall-out shel-
ter sing-song book, and official application forms accepting
credit card payments.

At the other end of the scale (unofficially), small home-
sprung bands tend to present their own rather less exotic

wares, i.e. a live-recorded album taken from a gig they performed at the Golden Lion Public House in Fulham, or possibly somewhere less exotic such as the Basingstoke Wife Swappers and SadoMasochism Club, Hampshire.

This whole business was summed up recently on a recording made by the group the Swagmen, with a song entitled 'When I Grow Up I Want To Be A Tour Jacket'.

MIDDLE OF THE ROAD   This term was once used to describe artistes such as Andy Williams or the Carpenters, but seems to refer more and more these days to acts such as Iron Maiden and Toto. This is invariably the fault of record companies, particularly the A and R and marketing sides, who because of some deep-rooted insecurity always feel the need to remove any form of artistic credibility from their acts and lump them together under some three-lettered description – MOR, TOR, BOR, RRR, Z-Z-Z! The list is endless, and even now there are teams of literary experts working on the idea of extending the accepted alphabet in order to fulfil the neurotic whims of these product-crazed predators.

Fortunately, there are still a few purveyors of good taste within the receding walls of the phonograph industry, and it is to these stalwart crusaders that we should raise our glasses and drink eternal good health.

MINI-BAR   Smallish safe-like apparatus installed in many hotel rooms by the proprietor as one more way of squeezing more money out of the customer. Contains a variety of miniature bottles of wines and spirits with an assortment of mixes and beers. The mini-bar's extortionate prices soon seem irrelevant when arriving back in the room with a new friend after several hours' partying. However, many seasoned travellers have found ways of refilling the used bottles with similar coloured liquids, therefore avoiding payment.

MIX   The surname of an old cowboy film star. Alternatively, a word used to describe the nightly traumas of a band sound mixer (a roadie with power at his fingertips).

MONITORS   Irritating speaker cabinets positioned at the front of the stage which often obstruct the fans' study of a performer's ankles, calves, etc. Originally designed to help each individual form some kind of balance within the cacophony of sound usually found in hard-rock performances, monitors nowadays invariably act as foot-rests for singers and guitarists. Advantageous to singers who need somewhere to stick their lyric sheets.

MUSO   Musicians. A person with the mentality of a serious musician. Not applicable to musical bluffers or poseurs (see Poseur). Most genuine musos are modest, honest, and totally erratic, qualities that do not always go hand in hand with the business side of the profession. (See Resting Between Engagements.)

Pubs and bars are natural habitats for the seasoned muso, as his place of employment is generally near, if not in, one of these social settings. He will, unless extremely introverted, become verbally intimate with anybody within a ten-yard radius of his position at the bar, but on closing time he returns to his home and becomes a very complicated human being.

'Our pianist always had problems with his electric piano. It was either electrically "live" or failed to work at all so that he spent each and every gig with a soldering iron in his hand while we managed without him. But the night to beat all nights was on the downbeat of our opening number as the curtain went up. As he brought his hands proudly down on his piano, confident for once that the thing was working, the legs gave way completely and the whole piano landed at his feet with a bang. He spent six months with us and he never played one note, so finally I was elected to sack him. He was upset and emigrated to the USA. He was lucky, as it happened, because the first job he got was with Jefferson Starship who he's been with ever since.'

GORDON HASKELL

NAME-DROPPER This class of person can usually be found at show-biz functions, bars, and backstage parties imposing on the company of famous people, who usually have no idea who he (or she) is. The said person spends most of his time 'dropping' the names of impressive 'friends' into his conversations in order to impress people.

NICKY One of the many words relating to cocaine. Comes from Niki Lauda – powder.

NIGHTCLUB During the fairly prosperous years of the late 1960s the northern working class were able to indulge in a once-a-week foray into the delights of the local nightclub. (Status could result in an even more regular turnout.)

The choice of entertainment was vast, especially in an area like the north-east where jobs were plentiful, as was the working population. Within a radius of fifteen miles, in the same week one could be entertained by at least three internationally famous acts. This of course led to a few repercussions, such as the compere who announced The Drifters as 'Four darkies, I don't particularly like them, but you might'. Or the doorman at the Shildon Workingman's Club, who, affronted by Del Shannon resplendent in a white stetson and Texan rigout, enquired, "Ave you got your card, and are you affiliated?' The anecdotes are endless, but the clubs have died. God help us.

'Name Dropper'

99

NIGHT OFF   Lethal, especially if one is a member of an established recording band. This is due to the fact that a record company will often arrange to take the act out for a face-saving meal and get them so plastered they forget to complain about distribution, promotion, advertising etc. Japanese restaurants tend to be popular for these occasions, and the dreaded saki once more rears its ugly head.

From there it's on to a club or disco with large vodka and tonics taking over from the saki. The debauchery that may ensue is left to the reader's imagination, but on waking later that day the dishevelled muso realizes that he has a concert in a few hours and he is unable to string a sentence together.

Feelings of panic and horror shoot enough adrenalin into the poisoned body of the pummelled performer to enable him to utter 'Oh my God!' before he once again lapses into a state of complete shock. Here the meaning of 'True Professional' will either come into being or fade into the atmosphere with the alcohol fumes.

In time, the performer will learn to insist on the 'night off' starting promptly after the preceding gig, and treat the 'night off' as an early night (see Early Night).

NIGHT OF SHINING AMOUR   A well-known event in the rock world.

NIGHT PORTER   The classic night porter can normally be discovered in the more 'travelling salesman' type of hotel, whereas a 'night staff person' is to be found in the modern up-market 'mini-bar in room' class of accommodation.

The night porter is invariably aged and suffers either from an intense hatred of people, or a life of loneliness. Therefore the character you will encounter on entering your designated hotel, probably at some unearthly hour, will greet you with either an expression known only to committed fascists, or a look of blissful fortitude.

Performers returning from an engagement are usually so ravenous that they will accept anything that is put before them. This is perhaps just as well, as the culinary delights offered by the night porter rarely extend beyond the choice of ham or cheese sandwiches. Lovers of draught beer could also be in for an early night as the bar is normally closed (unless the hotel is small and highly personalized), and bottles are the order of the night.

The more friendly night porter, quite often named Harry or Tom, will sometimes join you for a drink and prove to be invaluable company in these rather dreary hostels, whilst the miserable type will only enter on request, begrudgingly serve you, then slope on back to some cubbyhole to settle down once more to his book on 'The Horrors of a Tory Government'.

The authors recommend that whenever financially possible accommodation should be found in the 'mini-bar in room' class of hotel, but drink should preferably be consumed in someone else's room.

'The Alan Bown Set used to stay regularly on the outskirts of Manchester in the Mile End Hotel run by an asthmatic proprietor called Alf. He had great difficulty in pronouncing the letter 'T' so every time we rang to make a reservation, a coughing, wheezing voice would say in a broad Lancashire accent, "'Ello, Mile End Hokel."

Alf had a roll-up cigarette end constantly in one corner of his mouth which rarely seemed to be alight so we were convinced it was the same dog-end day after day. Every time he coughed, a shower of dust would erupt from it and threaten any passer-by with premature dandruff.

His favourite routine was to tiptoe past the guests' rooms in the morning, instructing the staff to do the same, until the magic hour of 9 a.m. when breakfast ceased to be served in the restaurant and the kitchen was padlocked by Securicor. Then at one minute past nine, all vacuum cleaners were switched on at full throttle and rammed against the doors of occupied rooms by cleaning staff who had been trained to whistle and yodel at the same time. Fully equipped with pass-keys, they would throw open the doors like guards in Spandau prison and inform the occupant that rooms had to be vacated by 10 a.m. Certain words not found in the *Oxford English Dictionary* would be our first response. Then after realising we had missed breakfast, even though Alf had sworn on his mother's crucifix that he

101

would give the band a 9 a.m. alarm call, we would search the premises for him to demand an explanation and breakfast. It was an old house and we came to the conclusion that there must have been a "priest-hole" or secret passage somewhere in the building because on these occasions Alf put the Scarlet Pimpernel to shame and could never be found. With the number of sausages, eggs and slices of bread he saved with this routine, we estimated that he could have fed the Household Cavalry for a whole year.

A plan for revenge occurred to us one night when we returned to the hotel at 2 a.m. after a gig in Manchester. Alf came down in his dressing gown to let us in, still with the dog-end in his mouth. He religiously counted heads as we trouped in, just in case an extra roadie might be smuggling himself in for the night without paying. Knowing his fondness for an extra few shillings we persuaded him to open the bar and serve us some drinks which he agreed to do in 0.01 seconds.

During the first round of drinks Alan requested a glass of milk and Alf, although very reluctant to walk through the hall to the kitchen (and unlock it), couldn't resist the 200 per cent profit and waddled off to get it, whereupon there was a mad dash for the bar, pint glasses of beer were downed in one and them promptly refilled by all of us leaning over the bar and feverishly manning the pumps in a flurry of arms and legs. When Alf shuffled back in with a glass of milk we were all seated in our original places quietly sipping our beers.

As soon as Alf sat down again Jeff asked him for some cigarettes. This meant a trip to the reception and another ceremony with the keys. Off went Alf, wheezing down the main corridor, again oblivious of the scramble in the bar as the occasional whisky topped up a pint, accompanied by muffled laughter. Alf had only one comment when he locked up after we left the bar: "Eee, you lads from t'Smoke can'k 'old yer beer. You gek pissed on one pink.'"

ALAN BOWN/JEFF BANNISTER

102

NIPS Yet another Parfittism. The letters stand for the Non-Improving Parfitt Syndrome and is what you get after a night of Double Excess – a day of Quadruple Hangover. As Rick explains, 'It is quite simply when you wake up in the morning, feel bad at lunchtime and carry on feeling worse and worse all day. It's those times when you've done too much the night before. Normally you'd have got better by midday, maybe even had a drink as a livener, but if you've got it really bad you just get progressively worse throughout the day. The only way to get rid of the Nips is to go to sleep because that's the only time you don't know you've got it. Nothing else works, take it from me. It's most likely to occur after you've done three days of gigging and you know you've got a day off on the fourth. That's the danger signal. Most of us in rock 'n' roll have had the Nips at some time or another.'

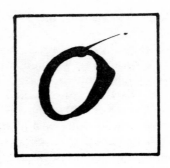

ONE FOR THE ROAD See Definitely the Last One.

ONE-NIGHTERS An ongoing string of single engagements booked by down-market agents with very little geographical knowledge. It is a well-known fact that some bands have, at some time in their careers, found themselves in Aberdeen on Thursday, Exeter on Friday, and Oslo on Saturday. One group was actually late arriving in Exeter.

OPENING LINES There are many legendary opening lines – an opening line being the very first thing one person says to another whom he/she has never met before.

The guitar-playing co-author of this book is known for his occasional uninhibited opening lines – i.e. prior to holding himself up by hanging onto someone else's trousers he was clearly heard to say to Pink Floyd's Dave Gilmour, 'Hello, Dave mate, lend me a million quid.'

Bravado Merchandising's director Tom Bennet on meeting HRH The Prince of Wales at a Status Quo charity concert in Birmingham in 1982 shook his hand and casually said, 'Hello, mate, where's the Missus tonight then?'

Opening lines are of great importance. Gaps in teeth have been widened and noses reshaped after an opening line.

'Hello, darling, my name's Dick. Do you like it?' or 'Hiya, sweetheart. If you like chicken try getting your lips round this. It's foul!' are both fine providing you are (a) a comedian on a stage twenty feet from the audience (b) a rock star surrounded by several bodyguards or (c) looking in a mirror.

On the other hand, 'Hi, everybody, nice to meet you. Can I get you all something to drink?' or 'Nice to meet you. I've got three Gs of blinding Nicky if you need putting in' will guarantee lasting friendship until you've run out of both money and nicky.

OVER THE TOP An expression not uncommon in the entertainment business as the temptation to live life to the full is far greater than that of the average chartered accountant or welder.

The telltale symptoms of this condition can be traced back to medieval days when court musicians had a tendency towards tights and brightly-coloured smocks. Nowadays performers such as Boy George carry on the tradition as if it was yesterday.

Fortunately one doesn't have to resort to such tasteless measures; the same state of mental affliction can be obtained by an over-indulgence in drink, drugs and sexual perversions. All three can be practised whilst wearing denim.

NB: When an artiste reaches this point of no return he is well advised to retire and write a book about it (see Authors of This Book).

PA   Public address system, the sound equipment through which the artiste amplifies all voices and instruments on stage (see **K**, Monitors and Mix). PAs have come a long way since the megaphone, although listening to some acts you'd find it hard to believe. After a lousy-sounding gig the sound mixer might well find himself, after the post mortem (see Post Mortem), with a ticket home (see Ticket Home) and/or a good chinning (see Chinning) from the musos (see Musos).

PDs   Per diems. A form of extortion practised by roadies and copied by musicians. The financial sum acquired is in respect of day-to-day expenses, such as food and drink, but is often used to acquire certain illegal substances, or cheap vodka.

There are, however, certain hen-pecked individuals who are required to abstain from such deranged habits and send their daily bonus, post-haste, to their rather insensitive spouses.

PERCY   Personal road manager. His title really belies his role, which is basically to be the tour manager's lackey. This class of person usually has:
   (a) a broken home
   (b) a middle-class upbringing
   (c) both, or
   (d) a background of lower working-class intelligence, and
   recurring mental illness.

His occupation is to do everything for everybody whose rank exceeds that of a roadie. He often finds this difficult, and is prone to drinking excessively.

'We were on tour travelling in a coach as usual. We always seemed to have the same driver, Johnny Sparks, a real Cockney. Nothing impressed him, not even pop stars. Every gig we went to he would pick us up at about 9.30 a.m., always the same time no matter where we were going. The reason was so that he could stop off and make a bet. The bookies all over the country knew him. On one of these stopovers Billy Fury (who was just starting to become popular) and his best friend Dickie Pride (who was a terrific, talented artiste although he never made it) were getting bored sitting in the coach, which usually meant they'd get up to mischief. They had cowboy hats, gunbelts, holsters and six shooters with them and were practising fast draws etc. I decided to go and have a coffee and Billy and Dickie went off in their cowboy outfits. The next thing I know, one of the musicians says they've been arrested. I went to the police station and there they were, sitting in a cell. It turned out that they had been walking down the High Street, decided to get some fish and chips, walked into the chip shop and held up the chippie, just as a joke. Unfortunately a guy in the back room had called the police because he'd thought the two were trying to rob the shop. I could just imagine them standing there in their cowboy hats trying to rob a fish 'n' chip shop! I finally convinced the police that the two really were who they said they were and hadn't been intending to commit an offence.'

HAL CARTER

PERKS   Gifts, tokens of appreciation, usually in the form of money, which are handed out to road crew members on behalf of the band at the end of a successful tour. Other forms of perks can come quite unexpectedly, such as the three days off in Hawaii during a mid-tour recess, or the striking up of a pen-pal relationship with a Miami coke dealer.

More realistic perks can come in the shape of some luscious form of femininity who likes your accent, although that particular attribute is not always appreciated in Durham.

PERSONAL STEREO SYSTEMS   A godsend to all travelling musicians and road crews, especially on really boring, long aeroplane journeys. God knows what they did before their invention. They probably made conversation, or got to know each other. Definitely better than Scrabble.

PHOTO SESSION   Generally speaking, a photo session is not something the so-called 'serious' musician looks forward to. A session can take anything up to twelve hours, depending upon (a) how out of it the photographer is, (b) how out of it the band/artiste is, (c) how many changes of clothes the band/artiste has brought.

With (c) some bands could have been in and out in twenty minutes but were delayed another eleven hours forty minutes because of (b).

Combinations of (a), (b) and (c) can keep a session going for days.

The cost of a photo session varies enormously. New acts

with no expense account will use a friend of the roadie who can borrow a 'good' camera. For the price of a pint and the promise of a lot of money 'when the record deal comes through' a band can end up with a load of rubbish shots which look as though the lighting was arranged by rubbing two wooden sticks together. This is the bottom end of the value-for-money scale.

At the other end we have the photographer who commands, and gets, thousands of pounds for one day's work. With masses of backdrops, assistants, cameras, lenses and quality wines in a huge air-conditioned luxury studio (usually in a derelict-looking warehouse in Bermondsey), even the shabbiest and ugliest of artistes can be made to look and feel like a star (for a day).

To bring the best out of a rock/pop subject, a good photographer needs to be able to pretend that the time-wasting 'funny' faces and incomprehensible 'in' jokes really are funny when deep down he is sick and fed up of these show-offs who lack the ability of the professional model to look great but natural in what are basically unnatural surroundings.

PICK   American derivation of the word plectrum. A small

109

piece of plastic or nylon thrown at audiences and sometimes used to pluck guitar strings.

PIRATES   Illegal merchandisers who, though protected by law, often come under the jurisdiction of band 'minders'. Upon receiving a request from above to 'knock seven sacks of shit' out of a pirate, minders will invariably do so.

POLAROID CAMERAS   Many musicians list photography as one of their hobbies and the polaroid camera is an essential part of any aspiring photographer's equipment. In a lot of cases it is the only piece of equipment. Used mainly in hotel rooms to capture that magical artistic moment with a new-found friend who was in the front row at the gig earlier on. The main advantage of the polaroid is that the quality of picture and pose can almost immediately be assessed and later passed round the entourage for criticism of lighting, subject etc. The more generous polaroid photographer will share his collection with unsuspecting commuters at airport terminals by subtly slipping one or two examples of his work into their duty free carrier bags in the hope that the works of art will later be shared with the innocent traveller's wife.

POMS   Tour programmes (see Merchandising).

PONCER   Someone who takes things from high-spirited people.

POOH-BUMS   See Groupies.

POSEUR   A show-off with little or no personality whose reliance on superficiality often gives new meaning to the word 'pathetic'.

POST MORTEM   Not of the medical variety, though a deathly air does sometimes surround the post mortem proceedings often experienced by bands after a particularly bad gig.
    A hyped-up and exhausted state does not normally suit

'Photo Session'

the atmosphere usually required in order to conduct a civilized and productive discussion. Unfortunately this exercise in negative temperament often results in raised voices and insensitive remarks.

After a successful performance, most entertainers find it natural to gradually unwind, say with a cigarette, a beer, or a quick albeit frantic search for a female form. After an unenjoyable show the above-mentioned mental and physical state results in the gradual unwinding giving way to a form of therapy once thought to be strictly confined to within the walls of a mental hospital.

Friends and business personnel, quite often unaware of the traumatic stage events, have become shocked and stunned on entering a dressing room which is shrouded in such a highly-strung atmosphere, and their satisfied and congratulatory smiles disappear as quickly as they do.

In most cases the problems are resolved as the adrenalin recedes, and the band will fight to live another day.

'At the Flamingo in '63 we were lucky enough to get Phil Seaman in on the drums. We used to get all-nighters there and at about 1.30 a.m. the band would start off really well, with some very very fine drumming. But the drums would get slightly more sparse and slightly more sparse. As we got down to one in four we'd be thinking that Phil was taking it very easy. Then it would be down to one in eight, and then the drumming would stop altogether and we'd turn round and Phil would be asleep in the middle of the gig over the kit. He never lost time, he just got sparser. We'd pick him up, carry him into the band room and lay him out. Then we'd go back and carry on playing without a drummer. About three songs later, in the middle of a song, there would be a flurry of sound from the drums and we'd know that Phil was back. In that number he'd play everything he'd missed in the three songs, he'd catch up, and there would be this incredible build-up of sound. This would gently die down over the next forty minutes – sparser, sparser, one in four, one in eight – until once again he'd pass out and the drums were silent. This used to go on every night at the all-nighters and it became almost part of the act. We'd have numbers with drums and numbers without drums, but he never lost time.

ALEXIS KORNER

PRESTIGE GIG A booking which is arranged by a new band's management for the purpose of obtaining something which will be beneficial and advantageous to the act in question, i.e. a record deal.

Representatives from the record companies will be invited, in a complimentary fashion, to a venue, usually in the London area (if the band is British), and be given drinks in a complimentary fashion, whilst being complimented, also in a complimentary fashion. The band will then take to the stage, will be analysed for 1.17 minutes by the complimented representatives, who will then return to the bar, have a few more complimentary drinks and bugger off.

PR MAN Generally speaking, the public relations person has only one real role to play, and that is to persuade the general public that the act he's representing is the greatest thing since sliced bread. He usually fails, but there again you can't make a silk purse out of a sow's ear. This kind of person needs good fodder in order to do his job properly, and good fodder usually arrives in the shape of some young, fairly unmusical buffoon who is willing, on request from the PR man, to dress up as a Hungarian transvestite, climb to the top of Nelson's Column in Trafalgar Square, and sing a medley of Tiny Tim tunes whilst painting his genitals yellow.

When dealing with the more sensitive, artistic type there's little more he can do but contact the regional tabloids and rely totally on the journalistic prowess of such publications as the Aran Islands *Shoe Makers Monthly*, or the Bishop Auckland *Daily Chunder* in order to put his clients on the road to success.

Financially the PR man (or woman) seems to do very well for himself which is not surprising considering the astronomical fees he charges for his services, and if one had to sum up this kind of person quickly and economically, one word immediately springs to mind. Bullshitter (see Bullshitting).

PULL   A willing participant.

PUNTER   Usually means one who gambles but in rock 'n' roll is the person who goes to the gig, buys the records – in fact, anyone who contributes to the upkeep of the music industry, and those in it. Maybe the word is used because the person is taking a gamble as to whether or not he/she will get his/her money's worth.

'PUT ME IN'   Drug related, meaning 'give'; i.e. 'Put me in' means 'give me some' (see Nicky).

QUACK Psychiatrist. A medically-trained conjurer who is able to put rubbish in your head and take money out of your pocket.

RADIO STATIONS   See DJs.

'At Radio Luxembourg we had lots of visitors from all parts of Europe and Great Britain. They would stand on the engineers' side of the big plate-glass window and gaze upon the disc jockey or newsreader. This particular night I was reading the news watched by a group of English Girl Scouts. Unbeknownst to me Tony Prince had crept in under the table without me seeing him and had tied my shoelaces together and unbuttoned my fly. I know this sounds unbelievable but when you're concentrating on reading the news you don't notice these things. So there I was posing and doing my best to look good for the Girl Scouts. I finished the news, played a jingle, introduced the next record. Then I stood up and of course my trousers fell down. Round eyes and giggles from the Girl Scouts, so I try to hide myself and walk away. Next thing I know I'm horizontal.'

DAVID 'KID' JENSEN

RAF   In common language this stands for Royal Air Force, but in this context it is a reference to that unsociable aroma which is known to drift unexpectedly from the dressing rooms of certain folk rock bands – real ale farts.

Connoisseurs will always remain loyal to this natural, wholesome, and hearty form of brew, totally unmoved by the comments of non-believers that the smell of rotton eggs is not always appreciated.

Many rock performers will refuse to be converted to this form of beverage purely on the grounds of vanity, as too much indulgence (a common ailment) in real ale can result in the dreaded 'beer gut', a physical deformity not in keeping with the general image (see Image). It is doubtful that any PR man (see PR Man) would request publicity photos which featured David Cassidy or Wham! draped over a firkin of Fullers 'ESB' ale.

On an optimistic note, copious amounts of real ale can be extremely beneficial in the making of 'farts tapes' (see Lionels).

RAREST MAN   Japanese nicky dealer (See Nicky).

RECORDING STUDIOS   When Les Paul first cultivated the original multi-track recording machine, his naive genius had, unbeknown to him, paved the way for all modern forms of electronically-recorded music. Not many people know that, but who gives a shit what Michael Caine thinks.

Good old Les, apart from putting the electric guitar on a never-ending road to success, he's also given thousands upon thousands of artistically inclined people the opportunity to enter a world of fantasy equalled only by a visit to the mythical city of Atlantis. Well, maybe that's a bit extreme, but so's rock and roll.

The authors will not go into a technical explanation regarding the development of electronically-influenced music in the twentieth century, as they are in no way qualified to do so, and it would be out of line with the general direction of this publication. It could also be incredibly boring.

To enter a recording studio, one must:

(a) Be a member of an outfit that has a recording deal
(b) Work for an outfit that has a recording deal
(c) Be booked by an outfit that has a recording deal in order to accompany said performers

(d) Be a recording engineer employed by representatives of said performers to assist in the making of a recording

(e) Pretend to be an assistant of said recording engineer, but be prepared to make tea and find fresh razor blades

(f) Be a ligger (see Ligger)

The record producer has been omitted from the above because his ego demands more than just one line (quite often not just in the literal sense). Nowadays producers are often engineers who have become bored and shrewd (there, that's almost two lines).

Recording studios have come a long way in just over thirty years – from Les Paul's garage (where visiting musicians had to climb through the window to gain entrance), to the latest forty-eight track digitally-delayed console in luxurious surroundings. We have now gone from 'Watch your trousers on that window latch' to 'I'll just have a quick soak in the jacuzzi before I over-dub that Chinese cymbal in the sixth bar'.

The home recording method is usually a two-track reel-to-reel tape recorder connected to various small amplifiers, mixing box, and effects pedals. Of course status can determine the quality of home recording methods. The wealthy rock star holed up in his mansion will probably bypass the reel-to-reel method and settle for a 24/48-track professionally-built studio with all the latest gadgets (purely for tax reasons, of course).

The demo (demonstration) studio bridges the gap between the original conception of a song and the master recording. This is of course on the assumption that the tune is accepted by a performer on the look-out for new material. People using this type of studio vary from the professional songwriter who is too lazy/poor to adapt his broom cupboard to accommodate electronic equipment, to local used-car dealers who wish to make their own Country and Western album for posterity's sake.

Master recording has now become an art form and with

the correct production methods it can enhance any type of performance. Unfortunately it can also make a mockery of human talent, especially at the 'pop' end of the sphere. Computers are now starting to be employed in order to reach a state of perfection that is dangerously inhuman, and should be treated with great apprehension. Les Paul, you've got a lot to answer for!

'In the days of 16-track, there was this elderly, very wealthy bloke who was paying for this young girlfriend of his to make a record. He was having the works for her. They'd just about finished all the recording – they'd filled up all sixteen tracks – and somebody suggested she should add another vocal to the one that had already been done. The engineer pointed out that that couldn't be done because all sixteen tracks were already full up. So the sugar daddy put his hand in his wallet and said, "How much will it cost for an extra track?"'

VIC MAILE

RECORD PRODUCER When George Martin worked as a 'house' producer at EMI's Abbey Road Studios in the late fifties, he was required to wear a white overall and was paid a set weekly wage, no matter how big or small the artiste was. How times have changed! In fact, Mr Martin apparently remained a wage earner through all the Beatles albums up until the legendary *Sergeant Pepper*, and only then was his request for a small percentage finally considered.

Nowadays, any renowned record producer can demand, and normally obtain, a nice percentage and a cash advance. Of course the record must sell in fairly large quantities for him to benefit from the percentage deal; as we all know, five per cent of nothing is not much these days. But a producer involved with a hit album can often make more money than the individual group members, as the band normally splits its profit four or five ways (unless it's a solo artiste, who then has to pay session musicians, see Session Musicians).

In the sixties, producers such as Phil Spector and Jerry

118

Wexler were admired not only for their inventiveness and imagination, but also for the quality of their performers. Such men were not commonplace. Bluffers (see Bluffers) often occupied the producer's chair and spent most of their time on the phone involved in organising money deals, dates, and other unmusical pastimes. The recession of the early seventies put paid to a lot of these imposters, but obviously they still exist.

Some of the better recording engineers have risen in status to that of producer, taking on a dual pole of producer/engineer. This set-up has often proven successful with many of the hard rock acts.

Attributes most common to successful producers are genuine talent, patience, understanding, discipline, and a sense of humour.

REHEARSALS Often looked forward to, but rarely enjoyed, this nerve-wracking part of a band's schedule usually takes place in either a damp-infested catacomb, or the sound stage of an old film studio, depending on the status of the act. Local publicans often become rich, and roadies often become bored. It's a time when band members really get to know each other, and unlike the recording studio, the work involved is quickly forgotten.

RESTING BETWEEN ENGAGEMENTS Out of work. The expression is exclusive to the entertainment profession, and more than likely came into being during the big band era when the term 'engagement' applied to every gig, and when out-of-work entertainers favoured a relaxed pose within an arm's length of the nearest telephone.

RETAINERS A form of moral blackmail practised upon dedicated backing musicians by certain rock stars and managements to prevent them from joining other groups while the former are holidaying in the Caribbean.

RICHARD Richard the Third – turd, as in 'I'm in desperate need of a hefty Richard.'

119

RIDER In theory this is a supplement tacked onto the original contract sent to a venue promoter stating the requirements of the act in order to fulfil the engagement with the minimum of problems. It will list the necessary electrical power needed, the stage size, the amount of humpers (see Humpers) to be supplied, what drinks should be in the dressing room etc., etc. To many acts a rider is a bit of a status symbol and in a way can be a gauge of the size and importance of the performer.

A new act will probably ask for a dressing room with a key if possible; a megastar will go for everything from the right colour suite of dressing rooms filled with exotic flowers specially imported for the occasion to so many bottles of Dom Pérignon cooled to the correct temperature, plus limitless supplies of top grade nicky (see Nicky) etc.

In fact, it's more often than not the dressing room rider which gets priority for some reason. The fact that the stage could collapse, the power fail or the punters be crushed to death sometimes appears to come second to making sure that everyone can get well out of it in comfort after, and unfortunately often before, the gig.

Most riders are compiled by the tour manager who is given carte blanche by the act whose only care is that everything runs smoothly. The tour manager, therefore, wishing to leave nothing to chance, goes well over the top in an attempt to make sure that he isn't asked for something on the night which he can't supply. He can waste astronomical sums on many useless and unwanted items, so a professional attitude must be adhered to.

In most cases the rider is straightforward, but there are a few examples of artistic eccentricity which are worth noting, such as the Bachman Turner Overdrive who would insist that a ten-seat sofa be supplied in every dressing room. Either the singer was very tall and needed to stretch out, or the band couldn't face one another after a gig (see Post Mortems). They also insisted on gallons of distilled water for some reason. Maybe it was used for topping up their rundown batteries.

Howard Jones, on the other hand, wears a glove. . . sorry,

requires, we believe, fresh flowers in his dressing room, well arranged. The ambience is to be one of sweet-scented flowers, not of disinfected floors. Also, as he and his entourage are vegetarian, no meat or fish must be in evidence in the vicinity of the dressing room area. This obviously rules out the possibility of encountering any disinfected victims (see Victim), boilers (see Boilers) or pooh-bums (see Pooh-bums), although the road crew must be grateful for their increased opportunities in this area. Maybe guests and support bands are invited backstage for a wild orgy of flower arranging and vegetable judging contests.

Howard also apparently requests on his rider that everybody has cheerful faces and a smile and a helpful attitude which goes a long way. . . Try telling that to Meatloaf or Van Morrison after a lousy gig.

It is possible that the Rolling Stones' rider is thicker than the Bible and it is rumoured that Emerson, Lake and Palmer based theirs on Tolstoy's *War and Peace*, whereas Don Partridge insists only that the gig be open when he arrives.

ROADIE   Not popular (the term, not the individual). See Crew.

ROADIE'S SCREWDRIVER   When something or somebody needs fixing in a hurry and everything else has failed, it is common practice for a roadie (see Crew) to administer a swift sharp kick to the stubborn object. A hammer can also be used but in order to avoid charges of manslaughter it is advisable to use it only on equipment such as amplifiers and expensive keyboards. This unorthodox art of persuasion is known as the 'roadie's screwdriver'.

ROCK FESTIVAL   The rock or pop festival first appeared in the sixties when young people felt the need to celebrate the 'togetherness' of the newly found 'pop culture'.

Jazz festivals had sprung up in the fifties, but the emphasis was totally on the music. Rock festivals, although usually featuring some of the best live attractions in the world, were to become more of an event. A happening (see Happening).

122

'Roadie's Screwdriver'

They also gave young people the chance to get stoned in a huge field instead of a grimy bedsit.

Though the novelty of those heady days of the sixties has worn off a little, regular festivals still attract thousands of people, and the sight of that denim-clad multitude alternatively basking in the sun and grovelling in the mud is still a sight to behold.

In the early days of the rock festival, the occasional young nymphette, probably under the influence of some new brand of Dutch lager, would straddle her boyfriend's shoulders and strip to the waist, while some lone zonked-out hippy happily shed his garb and bared his shrivelled nuts to all and sundry. Nowadays the fans prefer to cover themselves in layers of leather and denim, although it's pretty certain that promiscuity still abounds in the odd tent.

ROCK JOURNALIST   Of all the leeches, hangers-on, and general liggers connected with the rock business, the rock journalist is probably the most hated and least popular of the lot. The fact that they have the power to destroy a human being overnight (and often do) makes this species quite intolerable.

In recent years, that which was once described as an unbiased, critical review, e.g. 'The group's good, but it's not really my kind of music', or possibly 'The production and the experience shine through, though a couple of the tunes are a little weak' has now become 'This load of shagged-out old has-beens with their boring cliché-ridden riffs should be hung, drawn and quartered', or alternatively 'Eddie Vomit, the singer, screeches and screams as if in agony, occasionally mumbling some indefinable curse, while the rest of the band thrash hell out of the one and only chord they almost know. God, this is real, man, this is a truly meaningful experience.' And there is no limit to the depths of cynicism that some of these sadistic bastards will go to just to satisfy their frustrated and warped little minds.

On the optimistic side, there are the occasional journalists who can actually tell the difference between a piece of music and a tape recording of a live act of genocide. This class of person is very rare and should be treated with respect.

NB: The above description is completely unbiased and in no way reflects the personal feelings of the authors.

RODS   Rod Lavers – ravers.

ROOM LIST   When staying in a hotel with a big entourage, it is often essential to be able to contact other members in emergencies, such as finding your mini-bar empty at 4.30 a.m., or losing your itinerary (see Itinerary) at 6.30 a.m. which means calling the tour manager to find out what time everybody is leaving for the next gig. For these reasons, amongst others, the room list is quite invaluable. The stars will often be booked in under a pseudonym in order to avoid constant interruptions throughout the night from hundreds of fans who want to come over to the hotel and just talk for several hours.

'On my first visit to Los Angeles as a roadie with The Slade group, I was sitting in the Whisky-a-Go-Go with a few of the notorious groupies from that era when I was asked if there was anything I required during my stay in LA. I replied immediately, "Yes, I'd love an English fag." The look of shock on their faces was a sight to behold but worse than that was when one of them suggested I ring Rodney Bingenhemier, as he was the closest to an "English fag" any of them knew. Needless to say I smoked Marlboro for the rest of the trip.'

ROBBIE WILSON

SACK   See Amicable.

SECURITY   'Guttentag, Hans. Vas ist black und brown und looks good on das back of das rock fan?'
'I do not know, mein Herr Security Boss. Vas ist?'
'Mein Doberman Pinscher. Ha! Ha! Gutt ya?'
Security is essential today at most rock venues and in particular at the larger places where it is important, mainly for the safety of the artistes, that the over-enthusiastic fan does not get onto the stage. Presentation can take a serious dive when a punter hurls himself through the drum kit to get to his hero. You also never know what you might catch if he manages to lay a slobbering french kiss on you. The lethal combination of garlic, Pils lager, Marlboro cigarettes and goulash soup as his friendly tongue goes down your throat can almost guarantee a call for Hughie and Europe (see Hughie). Even less relaxing is the feeling of being scalped by Big Chief Two Dogs Fucking when one of the roadies picks up the fan and runs off stage with him to settle the score with a chinning (see Chinning), forgetting that the punter still has half of your once beautiful flowing golden hair clenched in his fist.
One of the big advantages of gigging in the UK is that the security people don't carry guns and teargas.
Yugoslavia, now that's another ball game. If you've never seen a baton-wielding Alsatian on the end of a gun-toting helmeted animal, try working over there.

126

Unfortunately, throughout Europe, with the odd exception, the police and security seem to have little understanding or sympathy for the enthusiastic, happy, fun-loving punter. Control usually works better when it's handled by the artistes' own head of security armed only with the threat of cancelling the show. If the kids aren't treated well they will quite likely crack skulls and rearrange teeth for no apparent reason. Maybe it's similar to the current problems at football matches, but what is sometimes forgotten is that at a football match there are two opposing teams, whereas at a rock concert there is only one team playing and all the fans are on the same side.

It's been proved many times over that it is not the number or size of the security personnel but their attitude towards the fan which can go a long way in controlling the crowd and helping achieve a blinding gig.

The harmonica-playing member of this co-authorship remembers well a gig in Melbourne, Australia, where the security consisted of all the members of the local boxing club (and many ex-members probably thrown out for brutality).

They were animals and from the first number Status Quo played they began the old routine of showing one another how brave they were by kicking shit out of a fourteen-year-old girl who happened to stand up and call out Francis's name. After many complaints by the band the said musician decided to get in amongst them, threaten them with the old cancellation line and try to stop them using fans as punch-bags. To his amazement he was picked up by four gorillas and thrown out into the street with a painful thud.

Despite his protests there was no way they were going to let him back in and only by breaking in through a rear toilet window did he manage to limp on stage and blow shakily through 'Roadhouse Blues'. The boxers looked extremely surprised to see this particular punch-bag up with the band.

Forgetting the boxers, Australia is definitely the place to tour.

SEPTIC   Septic tank – Yank – American. See also Sherman.

SESSION MUSICIANS   Session musicians are people who prefer the somewhat sterile atmosphere of the recording studio to the more virile type of renderings often associated with live performances. This kind of person cannot really be classified, as many of them will indulge in both fields of play, mainly for financial reasons.

A true and dedicated live performer will regard the recording studio with a certain disdain, but will also appreciate the fact that making records is a valuable asset to his career (provided that the recording is successful).

The old school of session musicians (often ex-members of ancient pop groups) usually look upon recording studios as factory assembly lines, producing row after row of re-cycled crotchets and quavers. They favour semi-detached houses in Finchley and have rather suspect taste in fashionable attire. Their enthusiasm for art is minimal, as is their contribution towards the latest Cornflakes jingle (see Jingles).

Optimistically, there are players who will give one hundred per cent of their time, talent, and creativity to session music whether they are ensconced in the latest forty-eight track, digitally-operated technical wonder, or some rat-infested hovel.

The days when a totally emotionless violin player would pack away his instrument and walk out of the studio because the big hand on the clock demanded so are becoming a thing of the past. Hooray.

SHERMAN   An American. Comes from Sherman tank – Yank.

SHITTER   See Pooh-bum.

SIDEFIELD MONITORS   Designed to make guitarists deaf in one ear.

SKINS   Cigarette papers used for rolling joints (see Joints).

SLIGHTLY CYNICAL   See Authors of This Book.

SMOKE MACHINES To the authors' knowledge there are two ways of producing onstage smoke-orientated effects. Firstly with the simulated smoke machine which gives the impression that somebody backstage is trying to burn a huge amount of wet straw. This oxygen-consuming mass will then proceed to rise and choke the band, onstage crew, and any member of the audience within twenty yards of the stage. Mario Lanza and the great Caruso refrained from using this apparatus as they obviously had the intelligence to realize that it not only knackers the vocal chords, but makes you smell like a big sack of burning wet straw.

The dry-ice machine differs from the former both physically and visually. Large chunks of dried ice are used to give off a thick dense fog which tends to hover at waist height, and with a less nauseating aroma. Its prime disadvantage lies in the resulting inability to see guitar foot pedals and monitors. Quite a few performers have earned their wings (see Wings) by stumbling blindly over these obstacles and disappearing, with a surprised expression, into the orchestra pit.

'We were rehearsing for the first night of a Larry Parnes extravaganza and it was Vince Eager's turn to do his performance. He got to "Only Make Believe" and the pro-

ducer started telling him to "Get out there to the audience, push forward". The orchestra pit had a pit riser which the producer had put up so he could work on the apron and talk to the artistes on the stage. Vince, in his efforts to please the producer, came right across onto the apron and the producer was clapping and saying "Very good, very good". So the rehearsal went fine. Then the show starts and Vince comes on and begins singing "Only Make Believe" – ". . . they think you really care, but my soul I can't deceive . . . but it's oooooo Aaaaaah!" All of a sudden there's no one there on the stage! The spotlights are searching for him and suddenly they pick up a hand coming over the top of the orchestra pit, then a leg (and all this time he's still singing). Nobody had told Vince that the riser wouldn't be up as it would let the kids jump onto the stage and he'd stepped out right into the pit. He got to his knees, then stood up and limped round the edge of the pit onto the stage, singing all the time. He really brought the house down, broken ankle and all!'

HAL CARTER

SOUNDCHECKS Meaningless exercises in technical and ambient matters invented by roadies who want to share with the band their misery at being stuck in a cold, draughty hall all day.

SPANISH TOUR A stressful undertaking, where the band (stars) are met at the airport by a fleet of mid-fifties Seat cars and taken to a hotel which is often 50–60 miles from the gig. On the way to the concert the next day, at least two of these cars break down and the artistes make their own way to the gig using the hitchhiking method (car transporters or Dutch hippie VWs).

SPOT (a) An act's position on a particular programme of events. (b) An unwanted skin blemish which always appears forty-five minutes before an important photo session (see Photo Session).

STAGE CLOTHES   Until the advent of such bands as the Rolling Stones and the Pretty Things in the early sixties all professional and semi-professional groups made an effort to look smart and presentable for public performances. Suits, shirts and ties, together with an almost military shoe shine, were the normal night to night attire for the average band. Style, cut, material and colour depended very much on financial status, but in general the look veered towards the smart, not the casual.

In the prosperous sixties most people found employment fairly easy to come by, so even the most semi-pro semi-pro band could afford one set of good stage clothes – except, that is, the down-at-heel college or art student groups.

Historians of rock have already informed us of the fact that the R and B boom was spawned by such students, and the reason for their somewhat 'casual' approach towards dress was purely economic. Curiously enough, there seems to be some sort of geographical relevance here, in as much as the London-based rhythm and blues band favoured the everyday 'practical' look, whereas the average Merseyside beat group always looked neat and tidy. It is possible that student grants stopped south of Watford, but this explanation is highly improbable.

The 'casual' look eventually came into vogue, and denim-clad individuals are with us to this day, inspired by bands such as Status Quo and a million others, counteracted by a million other performers who choose to be slightly outlandish. Stage clothes reflect the kind of mood a band wants to create on stage. Casual for down-to-earthiness, and not so casual for not-so-down-to-earthiness.

The guitar-playing half of this authorship once worked with a 'soul band' featuring the 'obligatory' black American singer. His mode of onstage dress gave the word 'imagination' a new slant, whereas 'taste' was somewhat ignored. Satin material is somewhat 'flashy' and, under careful lighting, effective, but does not respond well to body odours so it is often wise to stick to cotton.

Clothes maketh the man. If Liberace and Boy George are anything to go by, this statement is possibly incorrect.

STICK Aggravation.

STICKS Drum sticks. Pieces of wood used by drummers for throwing at the monitor mixer or the guitarist who has been giving him a lot of stick (see Stick) all night.

STRANGLE A DARKIE See Float a Log.

STRAPPING Large. Huge. Big.

STROBE TUNER A modern-day high-tech instrument-tuner which has proved that a harmonica is possibly not quite as precise for guitar-tuning as we used to think it was.

STUMM Pronounced 'shtum'. German for silent, but in rock and rollers' language, shut up. The use of the odd Teutonic word probably harks back to the early sixties when many British groups found employment (and reality) in places like Hamburg.

SUB An advance of money. A good way of spotting who's doing the most illegal substances. A good way of spotting who to ask for some.

SUPERGROUP RE-FORMATIONS A recent form of activity undertaken by rock stars who, in the pre-recession days of the 1960s, used to be regarded as immortal superstars. There are, debatably, two main reasons for this exercise in déjà-vuism: a) they need the money; b) they are finding it extremely hard to adapt to modern-day musical trends.

There are, however, some hard-core followers of this activity who believe that such musical second-coming is a natural progression. Indeed, this class of dedicated person should be respected, for he has declined to succumb to music of a 'lesser meaning', and also has a valuable sense of nostalgia, a human attribute that is to be commended.

SUPPORT BANDS People with whom you spend weeks,

135

sometimes months, sharing the same hotels, backstage areas, and bars, but as you've never taken the trouble to watch them on stage you have absolutely no idea what particular function each individual performs.

SWAG   Merchandise. See Merchandising.

TALKING CURTAINS   A term used by the first White-snake guitarist to describe the kind of bedroom drapes often admired by persons who at 6.30 a.m. like to gaze at the beginnings of yet another fruitful and optimistic day.

Though this positive attitude is to be applauded, it in no way compensates for the feelings of nocturnal creatures who, after retiring to bed at the crack of dawn, are awakened twenty minutes later by a spectacle somewhat reminiscent of that scene at the end of *Close Encounters of the Third Kind*.

Bright sunlight through unlined orange curtains does not give comfort to the soul at the best of times, but when one is confined to bed in a state of semi-death, it is even less welcome.

Suggestions for combating this situation vary from the hanging of thick tightly-woven blankets at the windows to sleeping in the wardrobe wearing a balaclava the wrong way round.

TEMPOS   Measures of time used in all rhythmic tunes to control the pace of the music. These should be strictly adhered to in all circumstances, but sometimes owing to an over-indulgence in spirits the tempo can become slow and rather slovenly. On the other hand, it can often be accelerated, but this is usually only experienced when the drummer wants to get away from the gig early (usually for personal reasons, and probably involving women or parties).

138

'THAT'LL DO'   An expression used by uncaring musicians which signifies the fact that the backing track they've just recorded was 'the one' and that the pub closes in three hours.

THE BODY   A term used to describe a certain black soul singer's stage attire while in transit. The costumes consisted of five or six personally designed satin suits which were much used and rarely cleaned. The travelling bag containing these articles resembled a sack containing a corpse in the last stages of rigor mortis. There are people who have witnessed the appearance of this spectacle on an airport carousel who still maintain that the command 'Come here' would have been obeyed if it had been requested. It never was.

'My band (The Rebel Rousers) were once gigging in Manchester, and after about three numbers I would introduce Roy Young, who would leave the piano stool and make his way to the front mike for a couple of numbers. One night he tripped over all the wiring and pulled out a connecting lead (one which pushes into another to make an extension lead). Thinking he had blown it, he gave one end of the lead (which was live) to Chas Hodges (who was then my bass player), and said to him, "'Ere you are, mate. Strip the end of this lead so that I can rewire it." Chas couldn't see properly on the darkish stage, so he put the live lead end into his mouth between his teeth and proceeded to try and strip the end off, thinking, naturally, it was a dead wire. There followed a massive explosion which blew up an amp, speaker cabinet, and knocked Chas onto his back. We thought it was the end of the world. Silly bastard!'

CLIFF BENNETT

TICKET HOME   Essential to a band member whose services are no longer required. Even more imperative if he happens to get the sack during a tour of Turkish prisons.

TOUCHING CLOTH   The sudden realisation that one has emitted a rather moist form of flatulence onto the inner

140

side of the underpants.

TOUR GAMES To relieve the monotony of the tedium usually brought on by constant touring, many bands develop their own in-house form of entertainment. In the more sensible and conformist set-up this usually comprises such traditional games of skill as chess, Scrabble, cards, backgammon (see Backgammon), and the more contemporary Trivial Pursuits. The less traditional tend to invent their own, more spontaneous, recreational pastimes.

'Initials' is a popular pastime amongst many musos (see Musos), and is a very simple yet effective interlude in a schedule of constant A to B travelling. Each contestant is invited, in a circumferencial fashion, to submit a pair of initials relating to a famous person known to the present company. This normally means somebody in the public eye through show business, politics, record breaking, or pure outlandishness. Indulgers must not immediately shout out names, but take a more subtle approach, for instance by asking pertinent questions such as 'Was he or is he a musician?' or 'Did this person invent a way of coating tadpoles with a small layer of matt paint prior to pre-sexual activities with an otter?' or 'Is this person still living?'

The common and vulgar element within the entourage settle for the clichéd 'Let's see who can drink the most Southern Comfort and spew-up' outlook towards gamesmanship, and are best ignored. They lack taste.

'Sticking different heads onto different bodies' is a lot of fun. It requires little ammunition, just lots of photographs, a pair of scissors, and some glue. The participant is then invited to cut the head off one photo and glue it onto another. If the heads are of people known to the indulger, the results can be devastatingly funny. The authors have spent many, many hours engrossed in this hilarious yet creative activity when they should have been writing songs (or this book).

Making up a complicated rock crossword which is then passed round the entourage to see who can solve it in the shortest time always goes down well particularly if the prize is a free night out with the dawn patrol (see Dawn Patrol).

The Small but not Insignificant Crossword

Compiled by Zak Starkey

CLUES

Across

1. Robert who knows the principle of moments (5)
7. Prince's downpour (6,4)
9. Wakeman journeyed to this part of the earth (6)
10. The condition of Quo (6)
11. George Martin's studio is above others (3)
12. Invisible to the police (3)
13. What Max Splodge does (7)
17. To knock down king or queen (6)
18. Blondie ate to it, Jackson did it (4)
20. DJ out of captivity (7)
21. Springsteen asks for a tent (5,2)
23. Traffic's lets in water (4)
24. Singular instant in love for art of noise (6)
25. Ad-dance, corpses are able to (4,3)
27. Seventies band featuring Tony Ashton, Jon Lord and Ian Paice that gave active life (1,1,1)
28. HM Band formed by ex-Scorpions, UFO guitarist (1,1,1)
29. You couldn't do this to an offer Mr Brando might make (6)
31. Mr Smith who sings from the big chair (4)
32. Mexican Rockers (3,5)
33. Is rap confused by coming in twos (5)

Down

1. Welcome to the pure sale mode (8,4)
2. Jay from Bucks Fizz (5)
3. Adolescent stomp from The Sweet (7,7)
4. Customers who push the boat out (7)
5. Punk's gob (4)
6. Drums that catch you (6)

142

8. Once more and once more for 10 across (5)
14. 21 across finds out where he was brought into the world (4,2,3,3)
15. Those who use are these (5)
16. Sade's gemstone existence (7,4)
19. 'D. RENT' as a style or direction (5)
22. 1977 Fleetwood Mac hit (4,4)
25. Hellishly condemned punk band (6)
26. Heavenly body Rod Stewart borrowed from Jimi Hendrix (5)
27. Townshend, Paul and Mary (5)
29. Diamond had a rambling one (4)
30. Clumsily failing record (4)

Answers on page 171.

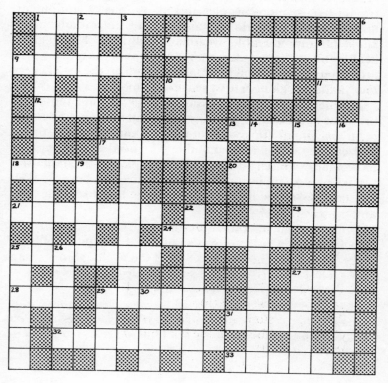

TOUR MANAGER   Loved and hated by all and sundry, and considered by most musicians in the mornings as totally inconsiderate for being concerned only about getting the show on the road. A whipping post, rarely thick, usually thick-skinned. Also, someone who you genuinely wish good night to at two o'clock in the morning when he's going to bed, and who you genuinely tell to fuck off at 8.00 a.m. when you are about to hit the pillow and it's time to leave for the next town.

As most band managers are not permanently on the road with the act, it is the tour manager's overall responsibility to ensure that absolutely everything on the tour runs like clockwork. Mind you, there are Rolex tours and Timex tours.

It can mean, on a big tour, worrying about moving twenty-five or more people, and many tons of equipment, hundreds and sometimes thousands of miles daily in all kinds of unpredictable weather conditions. Friendships, health and sanity are all potential victims of the touring syndrome on any level and diplomacy is high on the list of every tour manager, along with a sense of humour.

Minor day-to-day occurrences such as opening one's briefcase at an airport customs point and finding the excreta of an unsympathetic musician inside it can test the patience of even the most hardened and experienced tour boss. This particular example, although rare, is typical of the immature pranks played, under pressure, by the tired and overworked artiste who holds little or no respect for discipline and authority.

Once in a blue moon a tour manager has become artistically involved in his employer's musical development. Quo's bloke (now an author of sorts?!) and the Rolling Stones' Ian Stewart have played on stage and recorded with their respective guvnors for almost twenty years.

Hard gig though it may be, one advantage of being a tour manager that springs to mind is that he is always the first person in the entourage to talk to the attractive hotel receptionist.

TRAVELLER'S MARROW Known as traveller's for short. A condition also referred to as a bonk, a hard-on, but in this case specifically brought on whilst travelling. Often occurs in transport with reasonable vibration and most commonly discovered on waking.

TRUCK DRIVERS The grand old men of the road. Quite often ex-roadies who prefer the solace of their cab to the lunacy offered by gig wagons (see Gig Wagons).

TRUE MUG A rock musician who buys a guitar in Japan.

TWILIGHT ZONE SYNDROME Many members of rock and roll entourages have at some time, usually in the middle of an extensive American tour (see US Tour), woken from their slumbers and realized that they haven't the slightest idea where they are. This is mainly due to the fact that most Holiday Inn rooms look exactly alike.

Once the initial state of panic and confusion has settled, the now half-awake traveller will be able to deduce that he is somewhere in the United States. This conclusion, though of some comfort, does not altogether instil a feeling of security within him, so the obvious move is to call the hotel operator. The conversation that ensues will probably go something like this:

Operator: 'Good morning, sir, can I help you?'

Lost soul: 'Er, yes. This is room 162. Could you tell me where I am, please?'

Long silence.

Operator: 'Yes, sir, you're in room 162.'

Lost soul: 'No. . . No, I'm sorry, you don't quite understand. Where exactly am I?'

Longer silence.

Operator: 'Well, sir, as you're talking to me I would say, at a rough guess, that you're somewhere near your room telephone which is on the lefthand side of your bed. So I would say that you are exactly three-quarters of the way down your room, opposite a print of the Des Moines National Bank,

with the right side of your body perpendicular to a mauve-coloured lampshade. Does that help you, sir, or would you like me to connect you to the hotel doctor?'

Lost soul: 'Er, oh, no thanks, that won't be necessary. Goodbye.'

The lost soul then runs screaming into the hotel lobby and disappears into the swimming pool only to be fished out and led away by two large men in white overcoats.

UFO Unidentified flying object usually encountered unexpectedly at some of the more high-spirited social gatherings where the UFO often takes on the guise of a large cake or small peanut, and must be avoided at all costs.

ULTIMATE GIG One which is serviced by a great performance and a great audience.

UNDERBERG A revolting-tasting tincture, supposedly effective in combating a severe hangover but serving only as a quick means of reaching the state you were in originally. This small bottle of near-poison (reminiscent of syrup of figs) is usually found on bar walls tucked into the bullet spaces of a realistic looking gunbelt. Perhaps the bullets, together with an employable gun, would be of more use.

UNKNOWN WARRIOR An acquaintance of an acquaintance who turns up at some prearranged meeting place with something that you desperately desire at that particular moment.

UNTOGETHERNESS A most unpleasant feeling sometimes experienced by under-rehearsed bands.

UNWINDING AFTER A GIG Due to the amount of adrenalin generated during a performance (especially the high-energy kind) the performer usually needs to go into a

state of 'unwinding'. This gathering of one's physical and mental stabilities is universally accepted by everyone connected with artistic people. However, there are limits.

The sensible minstrel will sit down, partake of a pot of tea, chat constructively about the show, then retire to bed with a good book.

The rock and roll hooligan, on the other hand, will use this unwinding period as an excuse to get completely bombed out of his head, citing alcohol as the prescribed method of relaxation.

'In the days of pirate radio I was on Radio 270 on a ship which was sometimes off Scarborough and sometimes off Bridlington, depending on which way the wind was blowing. We had a Dutch crew who wore wooden clogs and whenever they were doing any work on the mast they would leave their clogs down below. This engineer got two six-inch nails and decided to hammer a pair of these clogs to the deck. So this poor guy comes shinning down the mast, puts his feet into these things and tries to walk away. It was a very funny sight, but it backfired because he broke an ankle and we had to call a lifeboat out.'

PAUL BURNETT

URRGHH!   An expression used by musicians on entering a less than desirable venue.

US TOURS   The doorway to decadence through which many an innocent soul has passed, only to return with the mentality of a crazed lunatic. The meaning of willpower is suddenly erased from the memory as mischievous boys become men, and men become mischievous boys.

The most striking aspect of the American tour is the sheer enormity of it all. The gigs, the food, the choice of groupie, and the amount of easily obtainable stimulants all pass before the stunned observer within hours of disembarkation. Everything is hugely out of proportion, but after a little psychic adjustment this can be used to gluttonous effect.

Hello indulgence, goodbye sensibility!

Status Quo fondly call America 'The Land of the Hefty Dumper' because of the unusual number of huge arses to be found there.

It's the land of opportunity in more ways than one. It gave one of the authors his opportunity to visit the home town of one of his favourite blues singers and hopefully pay his respects to the Great Man. Alas, on arrival he was informed that he had, unfortunately, just missed him by twenty-eight years, but a visit to his grave might compensate. It gave the other author an opportunity to develop his piles, which for him happened to be twenty years too early.

Travel is big business in the States. For a band of superstar status it can mean travelling from city to city aboard the infamous 'Starship', a luxurious jet airliner complete with bedrooms, showers, Hammond organ, bar, willing hostesses and designer parachutes. (Gucci sick bags were, unfortunately, optional extras + VAT.) From this these pleasantly pampered purveyors of predominantly perpetual and plausibly presumptuous pop disembark and saunter inconspicuously/conspicuously to the waiting limousine and/or man from Havana. This convoy of corruption then proceeds to the prearranged multi-starred luxury hotel where the suites, flowers, champagne and unlimited supplies of fun await.

At the opposite end of the scale is the band touring for the first time with absolutely minimal record company support. After their scheduled tourist-class flight they are usually met by a note from the record company at the message box telling them to rent a car at their own expense from the nearest rent-a-car company only thirty-five minutes' cab ride down the road from the airport terminal. A two-hour flight and five hours later they head in a very unconvoyish way to their motel where the sweets, cockroaches, ice-water and still unlimited supplies of fun await.

All in all, touring at any level in the States is easier and more natural than anywhere else in the world.

The authors can sum up the American tour in one word. It is: spasmodicallysusceptibletosalacioussituationssinusitistically surelyself inflicted.

VAN Transport used by poorer bands to carry the equipment, musicians, and roadie. Often doubles as a hotel. Distinguishing marks: stiletto holes in the ceiling and knee marks in the carpet. In the old days it was often owned by somebody's Dad.

VERMIN Noxious or parasitic worms, mammals, or insects. Also applicable to one or two so-called rock journalists (see Rock Journalists).

VICE-LIKE GRIP ON REALITY A state of mind not generally known to most rock musicians.

'Blackpool Night Out used to take place on a Sunday I remember and we left London on Saturday afternoon or evening. I was carrying all the luggage this time for some reason, and I had to have the boot open with a couple of guitars strapped on top of the cases. We got onto a little piece of motorway near Biggleswade and by this time it was quite dark and raining. I was passing lots of vehicles – in a hurry, always in a hurry – and I passed this big lorry. Then Ringo said there was somebody flashing from behind. I slowed down but this vehicle behind was still flashing so eventually we both pulled into the hard shoulder. Neil and I got out and went to this great big articulated lorry to see what had happened. The driver in it said, "I think you dropped a banjo back down the road." I couldn't believe it, but when I went to look at the back of the car the straps were broken and where there had been two guitars there was now only one. I distinctly remember thinking, "I can get a lift home from here." I said to Neil, "You better tell 'em." "No," he said, "you better tell 'em." So I went up to them and told them that we'd lost a guitar, and out of the darkness this voice said, "Well, if you can find it you get a bonus." This was John – I was always more frightened of John than anybody else. I said, "Yeah? What's the bonus then?" and he said, "You can have your job back." Eventually, after going back to the end of the motorway twice and slowly driving up each side we started finding little bits of wood, and then a guitar string. Nothing more was said about my job.'

ALF BICKNELL

VICTIM   An unfortunate young lady bearing no relation to the groupie type, who falls romantically in love with the artiste, and who respects him for what he really is. Unfortunately for her, he really is a bullshitter (see Bullshitting).

VIDEOS   This modern form of entertainment has now

become incredibly big business, especially in the pop music field. A slot on peak viewing time on television can enhance the sales of a recording much more than a spate of one-nighters ever could.

A popular theme for macho pig-type performers is to employ a couple of professional models to writhe about in totally submissive fashion, giving the impression that the lead singer's command is their wish. This is of course a complete fallacy. At the end of the shoot the 'subservients' order one of the band to obtain a cab and head on home to a real man. The chauvinist is then left to join his fellow bullshitters in a game of dominoes.

Another idea often thought of by video producers is to take the 'product' to an exotic setting, such as the Amazon jungle or a small Pacific island. The cost of this experiment must be astronomical, but the performers in question, spurred on no doubt by some deep-rooted Humphrey Bogart complex, suddenly become Hollywood heroes, and at the end of the day return to their camp beds with a complete loss of musical memory.

Heavy metal bands tend to favour the 'live' approach to their videos, and the inevitable dry ice expert is once again dragged from his tortured sleep to pump cloud upon cloud of sickening smoke on to a collective IQ of 35.

There are, however, videos of a standard so high that Hollywood moguls such as Jack Warner and John Huston must have wished that they had been born just a little later in life in order to partake more fully in a pastime with such obvious prospects.

VOMIT   This is a word used less and less in rock and roll to describe the ejection of matter from the stomach via the mouth. Much preferred are the more descriptive-sounding Europe, Hughie, Chunder etc. (see Hughie). The next time you find yourself with your head down the pan throwing up for England listen, if you can, to the sounds you make. The words Europe and Hughie are very close, which is where the immortal 'I'm just going to call for Hughie and Europe' comes from.

VOX   A form of amplification popularised by the Beatles. Also studio slang for vocals.

WAKE-UP CALL This exercise is carried out by naive tour managers until the verbal abuse, death threats and physical attacks become too much to take every day. The chore is then passed on to the hotel receptionist, and the now wiser tour manager sleeps with a smug grin.

WARM-UP GIG A pre-tour gig played in some out-of-the-way small town for the purpose of hopefully discovering the act's potential musical flaws and inadequate presentation. In certain cases the performers have learnt that it may have been wiser on reflection to use the tour dates as warm-up gigs and the warm-up gig as the tour.

WHINGE To moan. Some people are never satisfied, and they're the ones who tend to do nothing but whinge. It's said of one particular megastar that there's nothing she hates more than a good laugh. Every New Year's Day she watches four hours of *The Best of Benny Hill* so that she can get all her laughs for the rest of the year out of the way in one go. There are, of course, whingers in all walks of life, but it's the rock star who's become a millionaire in eight days and suddenly knows it all who takes some beating in the whinging stakes. Also a popular pastime amongst roadies to compensate for their over-tiredness and sexual frustration.

WIBBLEY-WOBBLEY MAN A person whose indulgence in intoxicants has become plain for everyone to see.

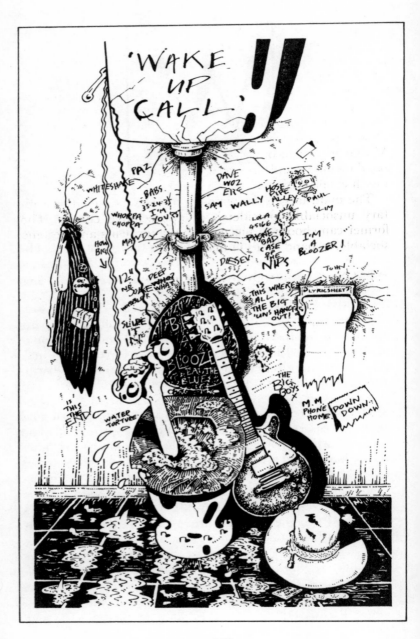

158

WIND-UP   A usually good-natured way of having a laugh at some poor unsuspecting soul's expense, normally administered to push back the boundaries of boredom often encountered on day-to-day, sometimes month-to-month, touring. Also known as a 'piss-take' or 'having a big of fun'.

The initial plot for any wind-up is quite often conceived by an individual with an imaginative sense of humour and an almost paranoic fear of tedium. Often accompanied by a Moriarty-type accomplice, he will strive to involve as many band members and road crew as possible in order to fulfil his mischievous instincts.

The main targets for wind-up merchants are either solitary unsociable 'outsiders', or appreciative clowns. The former can choose to succumb to the torments and become sociable, or hand in his notice.

WINGS   Another Quo-ism. Wings are awarded to any musician who actually trips and falls over on stage. Messrs Rossi and Parfitt have an armful apiece.

A smack in the mouth from the guitar of someone running towards you who only slightly miscalculates the gap between the front edge of the stage and your face can really help you gain your wings. Also a real hefty belt with a live microphone normally guarantees a pair.

Double wings go to anyone who disappears off the front of the stage into the orchestra pit packed full of photographers. In these cases the wings will be rushed by scooter-messenger to the hospital so that they are the first things the recipient sees on waking two or three days later when the life-support machine has been switched off.

'After we started working quite regularly (because our manager liked the commission), my partner Dave said to him, "Is there any chance of changing the act slightly, doing something to brighten it up, because I'm getting bored with it?" And our manager said to me, "You can do acrobatics, can't you? Why don't you do some acrobatics across the stage?" So that's what we decided to do. Dave would go out on the stage and say he was on his own, that

I couldn't make it. He'd start to sing and then just as he reached the harmony point I'd do a double somersault across the stage, land by the microphone, and go straight into the harmony, just like Jan and Dean. Amazing. The night came, the performance started, and off Dave went, and just at the right time I did my double somersault across the stage, missed the microphone, went straight over the edge into the orchestra pit and broke my leg. The manager of the club said, "Listen, can you do that every night? You brought the house down."'

DES COX

WONGA   Marijuana. Possibly derives from Status Quo's 1978 Australian tour which they billed 'The Wongalooma '78 Tour'.

WORLD'S SECOND RAREST MAN   A musician who doesn't drink (see Rarest Man).

Xs Expenses. The tour float (see Float). Non-recoupable monies paid out, generally by the tour manager, for day-to-day survival. The saying 'Let's put it on Xs' loosely translated usually means 'I want it but I'm buggered if I'm gonna pay for it!'

XYLOPHONE A musical instrument consisting of a row of wooden bars struck with hammers. Hardly used these days except in a book like this to help fill out the X section.

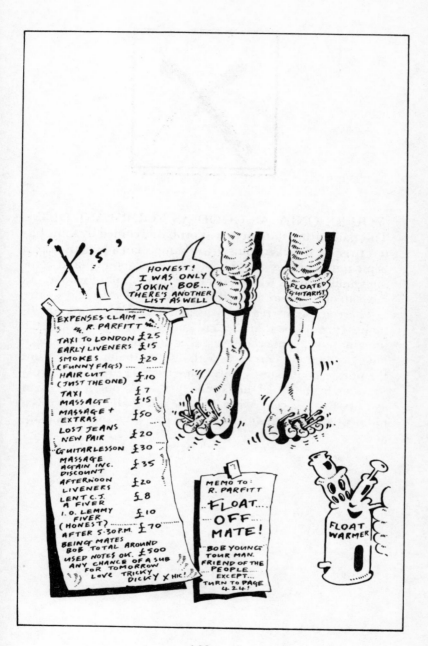

163

'YOU'RE ONLY AS GOOD AS YOUR LAST GIG'

This nauseating statement was probably coined by some bitter, twisted, drunken, out-of-work musician a long time ago, bemoaning the fact that there were lots of good up-and-coming young players who were better than him but who might have an off-night and possibly sink to his depths of despair.

There are many reasons why a musician may have an off-night. It could be that the hall ambience leaves a lot to the imagination, or maybe he's got a hangover. He may even have the clap, or a problem with his maintenance order, but the phrase could surely only come from a person with truly pessimistic nature. Unfortunately this accounts for about seventy-five per cent of the creative talent alive at any given moment and can create problems with wives and bank managers.

ZAK An extremely rare christian name which has been bestowed upon the eldest son of Ringo Starr – Zak Starkey, née Starr.

ZONKED See 'I'm fine, really', and Wibbley-Wobbley Man.

ZZZZZZs Pronounced 'zeds', as in 'Stacking up the zeds', or sleeping.

'I have had a blameless life in broadcasting. Very little has happened to me apart from disasters like *Blankety Blank* over which we should draw a veil, and indeed the morning radio show over which most discerning listeners draw a veil or at least switch off. But the other day somebody was inventing an amusing scenario about myself, David Jacobs and Jimmy Young. All three of us were dying (whether discerning listeners had locked us up and poisoned us in Borgia fashion I don't know) and we went to heaven on the same day. We were all standing at the Pearly Gates and St Peter comes out and he says, "Terry Wogan." I say, "Yes, sir, here, sir." He says, "Room 117." So I go to Room 117 and it's the filthiest dirtiest hole you ever saw. There's a dog turd in the corner and in the other corner on a filthy mattress lit by the one naked light bulb is an old groan with one yellow tooth. The voice says, "Terry Wogan, for all your sins but particularly for *Blankety Blank* this is your punishment."

Back to Jimmy Young and David Jacobs. Peter says, "David Jacobs." "Yes, sir, yes, sir." "Room 203." Jacobs is led to Room 203 which is even filthier than the one Wogan's got. There are turds half way up the wall in this one. There is no bulb; there isn't even a window. Filth and muck everywhere, not even a mattress, but in the corner of the room a naked old woman, a groan without any teeth, smiling through diseased gums, and a voice says, "David Jacobs, for all your sins but particularly for *Melodies For You* this is your punishment."

Back to Jimmy Young who is waiting to get his. St Peter says, "Jimmy Young, the Penthouse Suite, Rooms 723, 724, 725." Jimmy Young is led up to the twenty-seventh floor of this wonderful building and there is the Penthouse Suite with magnificent carpets, wonderful draperies, beautiful furniture, bowls of grapes in one corner, oranges in another, bottles of champagne, lovely bathroom, smashing four-poster bed you can just see in another room, and in the corner on a chaise longue, naked as a jay bird, Sophia Loren, and a voice says, "Sophia Loren, for all your sins. . ."'

TERRY WOGAN

CROSSWORD ANSWERS

Anecjoke Contributors

Russ Ballard, musician/song writer
Jeff Bannister, musician
Tony Barrow, early Beatles publicist
Jerry Baxter, roadie
Cliff Bennett, singer
Alf Bicknell, Beatles roadie
Alan Bown, musician
Paul Burnett, DJ
Hal Carter, musician/songwriter
Des Cox, singer/radio personality
Noel Edmonds, TV personality
Gordon Haskell, musician with Cliff Richard
Catherine Howe, singer
David 'Kid' Jensen, DJ/TV personality
The late great **Alexis Korner**, musician/writer/TV
personality
Vic Maile, record producer
Manfred Mann, musician
Peter Powell, DJ
Mike Read, DJ/TV personality
Martin Rushent, record producer
Jimmy Savile, TV personality
Robbie Wilson, former roadie
Terry Wogan, TV personality